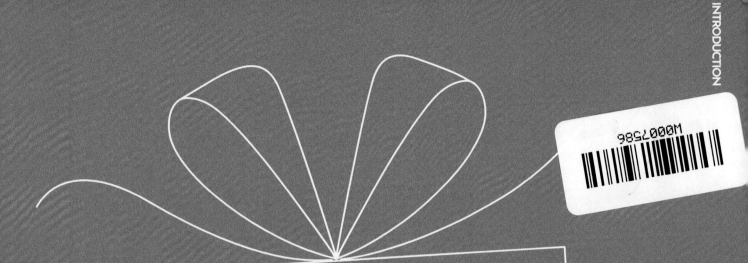

Thank you very much for your purchase.
It means a lot to us that you have chosen
our book.

That's why we would like to thank you with a
free bonus. It is a unique seasons-special with
20 creative Montessori ideas for all seasons.

Here is how you can get the free extra content:
Simply scan the QR code and quickly download
the seasons-special on our website. There is
something for every age group. The activities
train all of your child's senses
in a fun way, just like the great
activities in the book.

We hope you and your child
enjoy the activities!

~

GET ACCESS TO FREE
ADDITIONAL CONTENT HERE!

SYMBOLS

These symbols serve as guide!
They can be found next to the
exercises and indicate which area
is currently being trained.

Hand-eye-coordination

Forms & colors

Language & Listening

Touch

Thinking training

Practical life exercises

CONTENT

INTRODUCTION
0 - 3 MONTHS
3 - 6 MONTHS
6 - 9 MONTHS
9 - 12 MONTHS
1 - 1.5 YEARS
18 M. - 2 YEARS
2 - 3 YEARS
CONCLUSION

PREAMBLE

~

"I believe it is possible to envisage a new society in which humans will be more able because trust was put in them when they were children."

Maria Montessori

Montessori is as relevant as ever. The roots of Montessori education go back more than 100 years. But even today, its concept has lost none of its meaning or zeitgeist. On the contrary – the number of schools and kindergartens with a Montessori approach is growing continuously.

The basic principle of Montessori education is to help children become free-thinking as soon as possible. Someone who enjoys taking responsibility for themselves and others and who is independent. In this manner, Montessori education can be combined with attachment or need-oriented parenting approaches.

This book aims to show the basic ideas of Maria Montessori's education and convey the underlying principles. There will be examples that will enable you to practice Montessori ideas in your home.

A central idea of Montessori education is the materials children should use to aid their development. In this book, you will find many ideas to occupy children between 0 and 3 years of age. These games can often be played with typical household items you probably already own. Most other materials are cheap and available in most arts and crafts stores or discount stores, so you should be able to quickly obtain these activities, even with a small budget.

Most of these activities are simple in execution. As parents, your time is limited, so you shouldn't spend more time than necessary to prepare games.

Because your child's development progresses more quickly in the first three years than it will ever do again, this book is segmented into small steps and multiple timeframes. At the beginning of each chapter, there will be some information about the developments your child will undergo at that age. This information is based on averages. Some children may develop more quickly in one area and more slowly in another, depending on when these crucial phases appear in your child. Therefore, you should ensure that the games always match up with your child's level of development and interests.

This book is also meant to encourage you to understand this stressful time with toddlers as something extremely valuable. In these first years, your child isn't just learning to understand the world but also themselves. In the autonomy phase, which is often quite challenging for parents and was previously thought to be a phase of defiance, your child isn't working against you (even though it might often feel that way) but for itself.

Montessori education approaches small children with respect. It acknowledges that toddlers can often be overwhelmed by their surroundings and can absorb impressions like a sponge. Through tactful observation of their child, parents can learn how to cater to their child's needs and foster the child's autonomy and will to cooperate. Through daily life exercises, you can increase your child's participation and give them the feeling of being a valuable part of the family.

This book aims to give you the necessary tools to approach your children peacefully and at eye level and to aid their development to become autonomous personalities.

INTRODUCTION

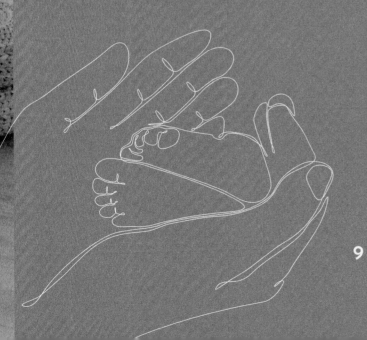

THE PRINCIPLES OF MONTESSORI EDUCATION

~

Maria Montessori was a pioneer in her field and created a complex structure with her education, the basics of which we will briefly explain.

THE SUBCONSCIOUSLY ABSORBING MIND

Maria Montessori believed that children between the ages of 0 and 6 could effortlessly and subconsciously gather and absorb information and are very sensitive toward their surroundings. The child then implements these impressions in their development.

According to Montessori, children of that age take in stimuli like a sponge absorbing water. This absorbent mind comes with a huge responsibility for adults, who are meant to be positive role models for their children. Maria Montessori compares this to a sponge, not making any difference between clean and dirty water – it just absorbs both. Similarly, children register, implement and copy both positive and negative behavior.

THE PREPARED ADULT

Parents and teachers have an essential role in Montessori education. Adults should accept mistakes made by children instead of correcting them, lead by example, and not disturb their child's concentration. They must free themselves of stereotypes about children and instead inform themselves about children's development.

THE PREPARED ENVIRONMENT

In Montessori education, it is the adult's responsibility to ensure their child can develop in a prepared environment. The adult decides on furniture and the type and amount of objects within this environment. According to Montessori education, a well-prepared environment allows a child to develop freely within specific boundaries. The child is independent within these boundaries and has a certain amount of free choice. This does not mean, however, that parents

give up all control. The child experiences autonomy in daily decisions. A child can, for example, choose the clothes for the next day but will select between two suggestions offered by the adult. The child can choose their own snack and select something from a fruit bowl prepared by their parents beforehand. We will explain later how you can turn your home into a Montessori-approved environment.

INDIVIDUAL DEVELOPMENT

Parents should acknowledge their child's development and not compare them to other children. They should respect their children's interests, way of learning, and what they want to learn.

INTERNAL LEARNING MOTIVATION

Children have an intrinsic motivation to learn new things. They are easily amazed, curious, and willing to learn. Parents and teachers can steer this love of learning to help the child develop their personality. Special motivation comes from practical and concrete learning, where children can make tactile experiences for themselves. They personally get active. This can nurture a more deep-seated understanding.

OBSERVATION

Observation is one of the core elements of Montessori education. Adults observe their child's actions. That way, they can recognize sensitive phases early on and some of their child's new interests, which they can then work with. Initially, it might feel strange to intensely and neutrally observe one's own child as it's playing. However, this plays a vital role in support and development.

SENSITIVE PHASES

Montessori calls times when children are especially receptive toward certain abilities or concepts "sensitive phases." This happens almost effortlessly. Grown-ups can recognize these phases by their child's strong interest. A baby that begins imitating syllables enters the sensitive language phase. A child that suddenly wants to do nothing but frolic about is especially receptive towards specific movement patterns. Montessori segments the first years into seven sensitive phases:

0 to 1 year: The sensitive attachment phase

During this time, the bond between parent and child is strengthened. Initially, the child is completely reliant on their parents. Parents need to react to their child's needs promptly and appropriately. That way, parents can show their children they are important and that their needs are being observed. A safe bond during childhood lays the foundation for mental health later in life.

0 to 6 years: The sensitive order phase

Toddlers especially have a high need for order and routines. Certain behavioral patterns are set, and things are assigned a particular function and a specific place. Children learn about logical meaning this way.

6 months to 6 years: The sensitive movement phase

In their first year, babies get more and more mobile. They crawl around, sit down, and may even begin to walk. This development continues in later years and is not limited to movement. Fine motor skills are also continually being perfected.

0 to 7 years: The sensitive language phase

Parents can assist their child's natural language acquisition by reading to them, telling them stories, and initiating conversations.

0 to 6 years: The sensitive phase of the senses

While babies mainly explore objects with their mouths in the first few months, haptics and looks become more interesting later. Toddlers are also receptive to smells and tastes.

18 months to 7 years: The sensitive phase for small objects

Toddlers love small objects they can carry around or put in small boxes. This trains their fine motor skills.

0 to 6 years: The sensitive phase of social learning

With increasing age, children begin inserting themselves into social groups. This time is a great opportunity to teach a child good manners by being a good example.

PREPARED MATERIALS

~

"Help me to do it myself. Show me how it's done. Don't do it for me. I can and will do it on my own. Be patient in understanding my ways. They might be longer; they might even take more time because I want to try it multiple times. Allow me to make mistakes and to exhaust myself, because that way, I can learn."

Maria Montessori

Montessori education is based on activity and material-oriented concepts. Child play is viewed as learning. Through fun, which the child feels when playing, they can relax and build their personality. That way, the child can create their identity. Playing should never be undervalued.

WHAT MATERIALS ARE THERE?

Montessori education mainly differentiates between three groups of materials. Here, we distinguish between language, mathematical and sensory materials. Developmental materials allow for practical playing experiences and involve all of the child's senses. They aid emotional and cognitive development. Sensory materials are most important in the ages of up to 3 years. They activate all 5 senses (seeing, feeling, tasting, hearing, and smelling) and allow your child to experience the impressions more nuancedly. Such materials have a strong optical, stimulative nature.

Practical learning strengthens your child's autonomy and gives them the feeling of being equal to adults. The already present need for movement is thus given a target, for example, when washing their hands or watering flowers. Everyday activities are carried out in a playful fashion, aiding gross and fine motor skills and practicing movement patterns.

Cosmic education has a high esteem in Montessori education. Here, the areas of geography, geology, history, physics, chemistry, and biology merge together.

Maria Montessori did not want to teach these fields separately. Instead, she put them with one another and thus underlined their meaning for the "grand scheme of things," so the world (the cosmos) and the interrelation between humans and nature are made clear. Your child will think about their surroundings and see their place in the world. That way, they will understand their responsibility for their actions and recognize their influence and impact on other things. For small children, cosmic education can, for instance, be realized with a calendar, through small experiments, or with feeling cards on which people with different skin colors are depicted.

PRINCIPLES OF MONTESSORI MATERIALS

Materials for Montessori education should have the following 5 aspects:

I.   The material isolates one aspect of learning. For example, it might concentrate on form, size, or weight.

II. The individual components of the materials are tiered and are gradually different. For example, the length of the edges of the Pink Tower's cubes is always one centimeter shorter than the previous one.

III. The toys allow your child to independently control their mistakes. For example, there is always more than one way of correctly solving puzzles or insertion games. If something is wrong, your child will notice and be able to correct their mistakes. This allows for a higher degree of autonomy.

IV. The toys are clean and aesthetically pleasing. In Montessori education, wooden toys are often used as they are haptic, optically pleasing, and also durable.

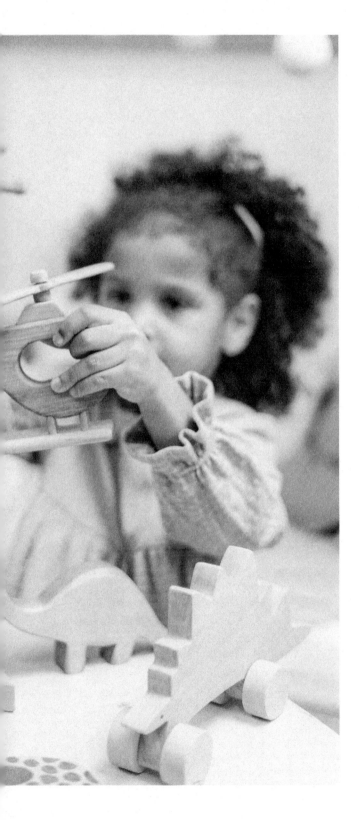

V.   The child can then work with the materials and is encouraged to actively interact with them. .

HOW SHOULD YOU GO ABOUT CHOOSING THE MATERIALS?

Parents and teachers have an important job in Montessori education: observing the child. That way, they can react to cognitive and emotional development steps early on and offer the correct materials to further aid the child. The toys offered should conform to the child's interest and level of development. Both are, of course, very individual. Parents should not simply follow guidelines but observe closely where their child's interests lie. If your child ignores sorting exercises, there is no point in trying them again week after week in different forms just because some guidelines say that a child should be interested in them at that specific age. Instead, it is much more rewarding for both sides to choose materials the child is interested in and will enjoy playing with.

According to Montessori education, a toy should not combine too many categories. For example, you should not offer your child a mix of too many colors and shapes. Furthermore, the toy should invite the child to actively engage with it. For this, puzzles, building blocks, modeling clay, or musical instruments are quite suitable.

Toddlers especially prefer concrete, three-dimensional toys which they can grab and use. Choose toys with a clear purpose. Cards with images are a central aspect of Montessori education. Especially with toddlers, you should make sure to use actual photographs. Drawings would require further abstraction.

You have probably seen that children often prefer playing with everyday household objects to toys specifically bought for that purpose. Real objects

13

of everyday life are incredibly fascinating for small children as they see their parents interact with them daily. The spoon that mummy uses every morning to eat her cereal is much more interesting than a fake plastic spoon. You can use this to your advantage and make toys from day-to-day objects. You can also fall back on natural materials. Children are surrounded by them; they are 100% realistic and from the real world. Children love playing with chestnuts, acorns, leaves, and so on. Don't be afraid of dirt or bacteria. They are also part of life. But with toddlers, you need to ensure that they don't put things in their mouths, as they might swallow them, which poses a choking hazard.

Be especially careful with tiny and/or sharp objects and sensory tubs with water. There is always the danger of choking or drowning. Never leave your children unattended.

HOW SHOULD THE TOYS BE PREPARED?

There are some basic standards that you must follow when making your toy selection.

» Present the toys on a shelf that your child can reach. That way, they are easily visible to your child, enabling them to select appropriate toys themselves.

» Order the activities by difficulty. This makes it easier for your child, as the order on the shelf allows them to simply switch from one activity to another should there be any problems.

» Always give things a framework. Present the toys that are related items in a way that they are also recognized as such. For example, you can place the rings of a stacking tower into a small basket and put the basket next to the tower.

» Invitingly offer the toys. The materials are meant to encourage your child to interact with them immediately. This will more often be the case if you disassemble the activities. So, don't finish a puzzle and put it on the shelf; instead, put the individual pieces into a basket. The same applies to any insertion or stacking games.

» Prepare the activities so that your child can begin without your help. That means all the materials necessary for the activity should be readily available, so your child can reach them. If you have a sensory table where the child's hands might get dirty or wet, make sure in advance that your child can independently wash and dry their hands afterward. This also includes the clean-up of any potential messes.

HOW ARE THE TOYS USED?

The interaction with Montessori materials should follow various principles.

» Give your child the reins. You want your child to autonomously decide what they want to play with.

» Do not break your child's concentration. If your child is focused on an activity, do not disturb them by commenting on what they're doing. Simply wait for your child to initiate contact with you.

» Allow your child to explore creative games on their own. If your child needs an explanation for an activity, show them the game without talking. It is difficult for small children to concentrate on both spoken words and movements simultaneously. Your child will be able to follow you more easily if you simply show them what to do.

» Do not prompt your child to prove their knowledge or abilities. Do not ask your child: "What is this animal called?" You should only ask this if you are absolutely sure your child can easily answer the question. If your child fails these tests multiple times, it might negatively impact their self-confidence.

» Tidy up afterward together with your child. Lead as an example. You don't have to immediately take apart a puzzle your child just finished. This might make your child sad. But you can put the puzzle back onto the shelf and, later, disassemble it when your child is occupied with something else. That way, you avoid any mess, and your child is familiarized with cleanliness early on.

» If your child has not tidied up according to your standards, do not shame them by re-doing everything the way you'd like it to be, but instead, make small corrections while your child isn't there. Once your child is in bed, you can prepare the toy shelf to be ready for the next day.

» When playing with your child, keep calm. See eye to eye. Even if your child takes a long time to complete an apparently simple task, you should not get impatient and give away the solution. Taking longer with an activity is a good exercise in concentration for your child. That way, they can learn much more than if you present them with a finished solution.

15

THE PREPARED ENVIRONMENT

~

"Not the child should adapt to the environment, but we should adapt the environment to the child"

Maria Montessori

A Montessori environment gives your child as much autonomy as possible and allows them to participate in everyday activities. That way, the child will view themselves as an important part of the family, feel valued and be able to develop a personality.

When furnishing such an environment, you can follow three steps:

I. Choose the furniture so that your child can be highly autonomous.
II. Recognize potential sources of danger and child-proof your home.
III. Offer the necessary tools to your child so that they can integrate into family life (for example, knives in the kitchen).

We want to familiarize you with some principles to create a Montessori home environment for your child.

» Your home should be tidy, clean, and nice to look at.

» Less is more. Minimalism means that you rid yourself of unnecessary things and only keep those that are useful to you or bring joy to you every day. Objects have a place and a function and thus will be valuable to your child. Order on the outside can follow the order on the inside. The surroundings are predictable and understandable to your child. Your child feels safe, and their natural need for order is supported.

» Buy child-sized furniture. Your child wants to participate in your family life and needs special furniture for some situations due to their smaller stature, for example, a suitable highchair for the dinner table or a scaled-down working area in your living room or the child's bedroom. The furniture should be durable and lightweight, so your child can move it alone.

» Look at rooms through the eyes of a child. That way, you can spot potential dangers you might have otherwise missed. On the other hand, you will also notice many decorations that your child will not be able to enjoy, as they won't be at the same height. Place nice things, such as plants or pictures, at your child's height.

» Offer a limited selection of objects to your child. Regularly exchange toys and give your child access to a select amount. You can set specific times for this (for example, by rotating toys every other weekend). Always keep your child's interests in mind and only replace those toys your child hasn't used. Also, clear away clothes that do not fit the time of year to avoid debates. Keep the dinner table clear of any unnecessary objects that might distract your child while eating.

» Create a yes-environment. It is exhausting for everyone involved when dangerous or breakable items are placed within reach of toddlers. Always saying "no" devalues the word and creates unnecessary stress for everyone. Place objects you want to protect from your child or vice versa (a poisonous plant, for instance) out of the child's reach or dispose of them completely. Make sure that the rooms your child occupies are filled only with things your child can touch without problems. A yes-environment will make your family life considerably easier.

16

The advantages of Montessori education are clear:

» Your child actively participates in your family life.

» You support your child's independence, so they can move about freely and actively.

» Your child's ability to concentrate is supported through minimalistic and neat furnishings with no overstimulation. They will learn to take more time for single activities.

» Your child takes responsibility for their own possessions and learns to be appreciative. They take care of their things and tidy up after themselves.

ENTRANCE AREA

It makes sense to place a small stool in the entrance area that the child can sit on as it's getting dressed. This makes it easier to independently put on socks and shoes. Jackets can be hung on clothes hooks at child height. Accessories such as hats, scarves, bandanas, or gloves can be stored in a small basket. The child's shoes can have their spot on a small mat. It is most sensible to only offer clothes that fit the time of year so that your child doesn't have the idea of leaving the house in a fleece jacket at the height of summer. A small mirror or some reflective foil, where your child can look at itself after dressing, will allow them to make corrections. A rucksack for your child can also be placed in the entrance area.

LIVING ROOM

The living room is often the centerpiece of a home. Especially with toddlers, storing most of the toys here makes sense. The adults will also spend a lot of time in the living room, and autonomous playing develops best when someone else is in the room. Store your child's toys where they are easily accessible, for example, on a shelf underneath the living room table or on the TV stand. Create a sitting area for your child with a table and a chair. Ensure there is enough light and your child's feet can reach the floor.

KITCHEN

Autonomy in the kitchen is very important for your child. Even small children can be incorporated step by step into kitchen activities as young as one-year-old. For this, however, it is crucial that the child can reach the workbenches. A learning tower can help here (you can find DIY instructions on the Internet). Use real plates, glasses, and cutlery for your child. You needn't use silicone or melamine substitutes, which can often pose health risks, especially with hot food. Your child will learn how to use utensils carefully and to value them. Store your child's utensils in a drawer that they can reach independently. That way, they can help to set the table. You can also use the following tips when making your kitchen child-friendly:

» Allow your child to help you prepare food. Toddlers can often cut fruit with an apple cutter or wave cutter. Older children can become accustomed to real knives step by step with gradually sharper cutlery.

» Of course, your child will spill many things over time. Give your child the opportunity to clean up after themselves. By storing a child-sized dustpan, brush, and a small cloth or sponge nearby, you can allow them to clean up their accidental mess.

» Make sure that your child has access to drinks as needed. This can be done, for example, by pouring water into a small jug and placing it on a table with a glass. Put a cloth next to it so your child can immediately wipe away any spillage.

» Place the snacks you intend for your child to eat during the day in an easily accessible tin or bowl. Your child will learn to ration these snacks independently. Do not refill the stash if your child eats everything in the morning..

EATING AREA

Whether your dinner table is in the kitchen or the dining room, your child should always be able to reach their place at the table on their own. There are many chairs for children with adjustable heights, which you can even use for toddlers with the correct attachments. Meals should be eaten as a family at the dinner table. On the other hand, snacks can be eaten by your child at their own table at their leisure. Children's chairs and tables are so low that even the youngest can reach the floor with their feet. Make sure your child's highchair has an adjustable footrest. Should your child choke on their food, it is easiest for them to cough the food up if their feet are on the floor or on a footrest.

CHILD'S BEDROOM

You can furnish your child's sleeping area in their room (unless you all sleep together in a family bed). Floor beds or house beds are especially suitable. Ensure your child can get into bed independently and without help.

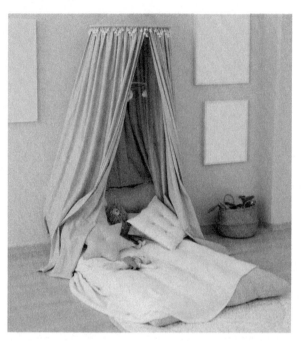

The child's bedroom can also be home to their wardrobe. Toddlers love to decide what to wear. You can accommodate this need for autonomy by getting your child their own wardrobe area. It should have a few drawers and a hanging rack that your child can reach. A large mirror or some reflective foil will allow your child to look at themselves in their outfit. If your child is still very small or is having difficulties choosing a particular item of clothing, you can also offer them two sets of clothes daily from which to choose. Make sure your child also has a place to put dirty clothes at the end of the day, for example, a basket in the bathroom.

BATHROOM

The bathroom is another place to assist your child's autonomy early on. Your child should be able to reach necessary items such as a toothbrush and toothpaste, a comb or a brush, and maybe hair clips. A mirror at your child's height will make brushing their teeth easier. Your child can wash their face and hands with a stool and an extension for the tap. This way, your child will quickly perfect their personal hygiene.

Most toddlers don't like having their diaper put on lying down once they've learned how to stand. From then on, you can rearrange your changing station to put the diaper on with your child standing up. As soon as your child shows interest in using the toilet, you can enable this by providing a stool and a special children's toilet seat. You can also use a comfortable potty. Remember to provide your child with access to toilet paper.

CREATIVE AREA

A creative area can enrich the child's bedroom or the living room. It should be a place for your child to get creative without limits. Provide them with pencils, scissors, stickers, and so on. You can also put up a small easel, hang cardboard on the walls for your child to draw on, or install a blackboard. There are no limits to your creativity, thereby enhancing your child's creativity.

READING AREA

A reading area can be established in the bedroom or living room. Here, you can give your child a selection of books. These can be exchanged in regular intervals for more variety. There are special bookshelves for children. Books can be arranged with the cover showing so your child can easily recognize them. Make the reading corner comfortable, for example, with cushions and soft fabrics. You can also place the bookshelf next to your couch or settee.

FAQS

~

Montessori education is complex and may appear hard to follow the first time you check into it. That's why we would like to answer some frequently asked questions that might come up.

I'M PREGNANT. HOW CAN I BEST PREPARE THE ENVIRONMENT?

Many new parents will lovingly furnish their child's bedroom. Here, you can make sure that everything is the child's height. Don't place wall decorations right at the top of the wall, as your child won't see them there and will be unable to enjoy them.

Kneel down or sit down on the floor. What does the room look like from this perspective? Is it engaging? Are the shelves on which you want to place the toys at child height? Is the room too cluttered? Is there maybe a plant you can look after later with your child?

Follow the idea of "less is more." Stick to a few select objects, don't make the room too colorful, and avoid overstimulation. But make it comfortable for you and your child, and ensure all materials and textiles are pleasant.

A child doesn't necessarily need their own room in the first few years. If you haven't planned a room, make a corner in your living room for your newborn, where the baby can explore the world for the first few weeks in a safe environment.

DO I NEED A LOT OF NEW FURNITURE FOR MONTESSORI?

Maybe you've seen the famous Montessori shelves, where toys are presented engagingly, or you've come across some furniture meant to give children their working area in the kitchen or the bathroom. You don't necessarily need new furniture for Montessori. You can simply create an engaging playing area in your living room. Maybe you have a low shelf your child can easily reach, or you can empty the lowest part of the bookshelf or the storage space underneath the living room table.

IS MONTESSORI EDUCATION STILL CURRENT AND RELEVANT?

The pedagogy of Maria Montessori is more than 100 years old. But her way of allowing children to develop freely in a prepared environment is as current as ever. The number of Montessori kindergartens and schools is growing continuously. Also, modern brain research shows that many things Maria Montessori observed can also be seen in brain development. Bioneural research shows that learning is aided by independent activity. The famous neuroscientist Manfred Spitzer also speaks of timeframes or critical periods in which specific behaviors can be learned more easily. If you miss this timeframe, it will be much more challenging, for example, to learn the language. Spitzer also says that children need various offerings for their age to make their experiences. The adults' job is to offer these stimuli and opportunities to learn. The exercises and repetitions with Montessori materials are verified by modern learning research. The synapses in our brain extend further and further the more often we repeat a certain thing. "Practice makes perfect" isn't just an old saying but is founded in science. Montessori is more current than ever before.

HOW CAN I USE MONTESSORI IN MY EVERYDAY LIFE?

Montessori education is mainly about a mindset that allows your child to become autonomous and independent early on, staying true to the motto "help me help myself." This can come up in everyday life in various ways. You can rearrange your home so your child can be autonomous despite their height, for example, with the help of a learning tower in the kitchen or a wardrobe where they can get changed without your help. Especially your child's play area or bedroom should be adjusted to their height.

Skills that your child needs for early independence can be learned in a playful way. The game ideas in this book aim to support your child's autonomy from an early age.

THE PLACE WE LIVE IS VERY SMALL. DOES IT STILL MAKE SENSE TO FOLLOW MONTESSORI?

Montessori education aims to turn your child into an independent, confident, and responsible person. Yes, Montessori makes sense even in the smallest of homes. Even in small spaces, there are ways for your child to act independently. Maybe you just need to be a little more creative.

Wardrobes are often constructed with few materials, and DIY versions are often more room-saving than pre-made models. Even in a tiny bathroom, you can create a washing area for your child, perhaps behind the door or on a wall with suction cups or in the bathtub. Your child doesn't need a children's kitchen if you don't have the space for it. . You can just work together at the kitchen table, the learning tower, or the worktop. You can still place a basket for your child's clothes or find a place to put away their shoes in a small hallway or landing.

WHAT KIND OF CHILDREN IS MONTESSORI SUITABLE FOR, AND WHEN IS IT UNSUITABLE?

Generally speaking, Montessori is suitable for most children. The idea is to allow children to develop freely in a prepared environment. Children are born curious and can live out this fact through Montessori education.

You can adjust the framework so that it fits your child. A child who has difficulties concentrating on exercises might not need a lot of things offered to them at the same time. With children that are currently testing their boundaries, you can work with a yes-environment.

Yet, some children might be overwhelmed with the freedom and selection. This often shows in school. Some parents ask whether their child is really suited to this learning environment. The fact is, every child can learn to deal with freedom of choice; some just need their hands to be held a little more. Here the adults must observe well and give the child the help they need if it is evident that they are completely overwhelmed. And with Maria Montessori, the adults set the framework where the child can move freely in a safe and structured place.

The more important question is: what kind of parents is Montessori suitable for?

If it's important to you that your children learn at the same speed that most other children learn, or if you like to compare or need lots of reassurance from outside to ensure that your child is learning well enough, then the free and more observant way might not be the one for you.

ARE MONTESSORI TOYS EXPENSIVE?

Montessori education uses toys made out of natural materials, preferably wood. These can be pretty expensive and have become more so recently due to scarcity of resources and inflation.

The good news is you don't have to buy many Montessori toys. With suitable materials, you can build your own. You'll be surprised how many materials you already have at home or can buy cheaply in arts and crafts stores. You can get creative.

If you want to buy toys with limited financial resources, buying what you know your child will enjoy for a long time is best. You can use silk cloths for many game ideas for babies, and even when your child is older, they will still enjoy it, like when the green cloth becomes a pasture within the world your child has thought up. Many toys can also be bought in good condition on the Internet or at garage sales and flea markets.

AM I NEVER SUPPOSED TO BUY TOYS MADE FROM PLASTIC EVER AGAIN?

Please don't think of Montessori education as being limiting. Regular toys and Montessori don't exclude each other. Nowadays, most parents won't structure the whole day according to Montessori principles and only use select materials. But you can still keep Montessori in mind when choosing the toys. For example, buy Lego sets that depict real-life situations rather than those that play in fantasy worlds. Of course, you can also purchase plastic toys or some sought-after merchandise.

Often, but not always, you can find the same toys made out of wood. These are usually more expensive than their plastic counterparts. Still, it's a good investment, especially if it's something your child will enjoy for a long time. You can also make many toys yourself from regular household items. This book showcases many such ideas.

WHAT ARE TOY ROTATIONS ALL ABOUT?

In Montessori education, we avoid giving children too many toys at once. Children with lots of toys at their disposal usually engage in one activity for a shorter time. Instead, give them fewer toys and regularly swap them out. Your child will play with the individual toys for longer.

Keep your child's interests in mind. Toys that haven't been played with in a week can be put away. Instead, offer something else. It makes sense to rotate like this when your child isn't there, for example, when asleep.

You decide how often to rotate toys. Usually, this happens after one or two weeks, but you can adapt to the current situation.

WHERE DO I KEEP UNUSED TOYS?

It makes sense to store them in a place your child can't access. That way, they can't sneak away unnoticed, grab some of the toys and create chaos.

Keep the packaging of all the toys. That way, you won't lose any small parts when putting them away. Original packaging is always a plus if you plan to sell them once your child has grown out of them. If you've made something, you can store it in envelopes or small boxes. Label them properly so you always know where to find everything.

HOW CAN I PRESENT TOYS IN AN ENGAGING WAY?

Your child should be able to see and easily reach all the toys. Place the materials at your child's height. Put heavy things at the bottom and lighter items at the top, ordered by difficulty.

The toys should be inviting. Don't store puzzles while they're finished; put the individual parts into a small basket instead.

HOW CAN I ENSURE ORDER?

Due to the reduced number of toys, there usually isn't too much chaos. Create a framework for playing and avoid leaving single parts lying around. You can find many cheap, small, and large baskets in various stores, which you can use for baby toys. You can store the toys easily visible and tidily. For larger toys, you can use small wooden tables.

Always tidy up after playing with your child. A toy that you've finished with is always put back in its place afterward. You will be amazed how quickly your child will copy this behavior and help you tidy up. Lead by example from a young age.

MY CHILD ISN'T USING THE TOYS THE WAY I IMAGINED. I'M FRUSTRATED. WHAT CAN I DO?

Free yourself of the notion that your child must play with toys in a "correct" way. The toy offers are simply that - offers. If your child doesn't want to use them for their intended purpose but would rather do something else with them, that's okay. If this happens regularly, you can ask yourself if the toys fit your child's level of development or if they're too easy or too complicated, and if that's why they're so often "misused." If your child ignores some of the offers and won't use them, just put them away and observe your child's current interests.

MY CHILD IS BEING CARED FOR IN A NURSERY. THEY ARE NOT A MONTESSORI NURSERY. DOES IT STILL MAKE SENSE TO DO IT AT HOME?

Most parents will realize at some point that, in certain situations, their child is confronted with educational methods that are a little or very different compared to what they are practicing. If you're going by Montessori at home, your child will still benefit from it, even if they spend eight hours a day in kindergarten or a nursery. Montessori does not have to be practiced 24 hours a day. It's about the idea of seeing your child as an independent and autonomous person from an early age and supporting this autonomy. This can still be practiced, no matter how the child is otherwise educated.

Montessori has found its way into most kindergartens and nurseries. Maybe they don't all have Montessori materials, and the caregivers and teachers might not be experts. Still, the modern way is to be participatory and at eye level with the child. Thus, nurseries have internalized the most important aspect. Furthermore, your child will also profit from seeing other education methods, for example, with their grandpa-

rents. That way, children will get a sense that every person's boundaries and expectations are different. Children can generally cope very well with it; they just have to find out what's important to them for every adult and situation. Then the children can react to the various rules. It only becomes difficult once one person changes their demeanor multiple times.

DO YOU REALLY NEED MONTESSORI TO HELP WITH CREATIVITY AND AUTONOMY?

The way of Montessori is one of many that you, as parents, can take. Even without a Montessori education, children can become creative and independent. However, Maria Montessori's idea can help your child find self-efficacy and develop the wish to care for themselves and others from an early age.

WHAT IF I CAN'T ALWAYS KEEP TO THE WAYS OF MONTESSORI?

As stated before, the most essential part is your mindset. Stick to it and live it with conviction. It's not a problem if you forget your toy rotation, leave the child's bedroom the way it is for a while, or don't have anything new to offer your child for some time. You're only human, don't overdo it. If you give your children new materials but are stressed at the same time, they won't really benefit from that.

WHAT IF MY CHILD WON'T TAKE TO ONE OF THE IDEAS FROM THE BOOK?

The clear answer is that you shouldn't overwhelm your child. Your child doesn't have to be perfect at everything or enjoy everything. Children choose their interests and what they want to learn. You give them ideas. If you see that your child just can't get dressed by themselves yet or doesn't want to because they haven't quite got the motor skills yet, it's your job to help and be there as a parent. You must also differentiate between autonomy and abandonment. Sometimes children just want you to do things for them, even though they could do them without help. Especially when getting dressed, a considerable relationship component comes with it. Your child enjoys it when you help and take care of them. Find the best compromise, and don't always insist that your child must do everything independently, even if they can.

DO I HAVE TO ALLOW MY CHILD TO DO EVERYTHING?

There is a definite answer here: no! You should, however, combine Montessori with a need and attachment-oriented relationship. Take your child seriously and see them as equal. Set boundaries where necessary and trust in your adult mind. Keep your own boundaries in mind and explain them to your child in a friendly but assertive manner. When the child is older, you can make some rules. This usually doesn't work with toddlers, but you can always explain them. Also, accepting a friendly "no" is a part of life and must be learned.

SO, HOW DO I WORK WITH THIS BOOK?

You can look at the Montessori approach and the ideas in this book as a kind of buffet, where you can pick and choose what fits you and your family and would help you in your daily lives. Don't overwhelm your child or yourself. Question and observe yourself and your child and pick out what's best for everyone involved.

ZERO TO THREE MONTHS

~

At this stage, your child does not need many toys. Instead, the child must learn the boundaries of their own body and will experience many environmental influences for the first time. Initially, your child will sleep most of the time, but after a while, they will begin showing interest in their surroundings. You can help by offering stimuli that won't overwhelm your child while still gaining interest.

Motor development: In the first three months, your baby will learn to keep their head upright and control its torso. In the first two months, your baby's hands will mainly be clenched into fists, and due to the grabbing reflex, they will grab anything you give them. In the third month, the hands are more open. Your child can now consciously hold objects and lead them to their mouth. You can support your child by offering grabbing toys.

Sensory development: Babies can only see clearly for a distance of about 30 cm after birth. That is how far a mother's face is away from her baby when feeding it. In the beginning, babies can almost only see black and white (although a preference for red has been observed in some babies), and they can distinguish between light and dark. At two months, your baby develops a sense of colors and can perceive stark contrasts and primary colors. At three months, your baby can see clearly at a distance of two and a half meters.

The mobiles in this chapter are based on your child's vision in the first three months of life. They focus exclusively on black-and-white contrasts in the beginning and on dazzling primary colors later on. You can adapt homemade mobiles to your child's stage of development by buying a wooden toy arch that does not have anything attached to it yet. If you have already received a toy arch as a gift from a relative, you can simply cut off the strings and repaint it in a neutral shade of wood, if necessary, so that the child's attention is focused on the mobile in question without distraction.

Cognitive and relational development: Babies must learn to adapt to their environment after birth. This adaptation is facilitated by reflexes, most of which disappear within the first three months. The baby communicates by crying and can thus tell what they like and dislike from the second month of life. At about four weeks, the conscious smile develops. In the first three months of life, your child also develops their first day-night rhythm.

MOBILES

In Montessori education, mobiles are neither meant as a distraction nor a sleep aid. Instead, they allow a newborn baby to engage with their surroundings. That is why you should not hang mobiles above the bed or changing table, but instead above the playing area, for example, in the living room. There, your child can move freely. Place your child underneath the mobile when they are awake and attentive.

THE MUNARI MOBILE

The Munari mobile uses clear, geometric shapes and black-and-white contrasts. You can easily make this mobile and only need black and white construction paper and a transparent ball with a hook. You will find many free printing and building instructions on the Internet, but you can also buy them pre-made on sites like Etsy.

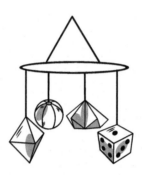

When? From birth.
Time needed: an hour
Preparation: Medium
What does this support? Concentration, eyesight
Materials: black and white construction paper, a transparent ball with a hook

CONTRAST PICTURES

When? From 3 weeks.
What does this support? Perception of contrasts and some details

Babies love stark contrasts. You can show these to your baby not only through a mobile but also with contrast cards. It's important that there is only one image per side or card, for example, a black animal on a white background without many details. These contrast images can then be attached to the playing arch as a mobile with some string or put up against the wall. There are printing templates on the Internet (often for free), and you can even get complete contrast books.

We have already prepared free contrast cards for you to print at home:

CONTRAST BALLS

Using simple patterns, such as repeating black and white stripes, black stripes, red dots, etc., you can paint large, white Styrofoam balls or transparent baubles with high-contrast colors (preferably black, white, and red). Do not overwhelm your child with a wild mix of patterns. You can place the balls at different heights to make everything more interesting.

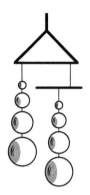

When? From 4 weeks.
Time needed: an hour
Preparation: Medium
What does this support? Concentration, perception of primary color red
Materials: Styrofoam balls or transparent balls, colors

When? From 5 weeks.
Time needed: an hour
Preparation: Medium
What does this support? Perception of primary colors, stereoscopic vision
Materials: Metallic construction paper

THE OCTAHEDRON MOBILE

The octahedrons are made from equilateral, metallic, and shimmering triangles and are often made using metallic construction paper. The octahedrons are placed at different heights. Your baby can easily see the shining, shimmering colors and will watch the mobile with interest. Make sure to use only one color per octahedron to not overstimulate your child.

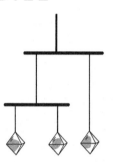

THE GOBBI MOBILE

This mobile consists of five balls arranged next to each other and wrapped in knitting yarn. For this, you can use commercially available Styrofoam balls (diameter of approximately 4 cm). These are very light and therefore move even with a slight breeze. This will make them all the more interesting for your child.

The mobile is meant to show your child the different shades of color. So, use knitting yarn of the same color family, for example, different shades of blue. The darkest colored ball would be the lowest and the lightest at the top. This will make it more interesting to the child.

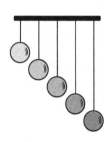

When? From 8 weeks.
Time needed: an hour
Preparation: Medium
What does this support? Perception of color grades
Materials: Styrofoam balls, knitting yarn

GRABBING TOYS

When? From 4 weeks.
Time needed:
5 Minutes
Preparation: Easy
What does this support? Open hand position, attempts to grasp
Materials: Ribbons

GRABBING EXERCISES ON THE PLAYING ARCH

Knot ribbons (gift ribbons) at the top of the playing arch. Your baby will enjoy the different colors and try to grasp the ribbons.

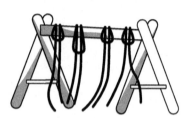

GRABBING RINGS

There are many wooden grab rings available for a minimal price. If you like handicrafts, you can crochet around wooden beads, then thread them on and close them to form a ring. Make sure to use baby wool. You can crochet a small bell into the ring to make it even more interesting.

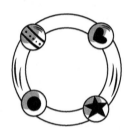

When? From 6 weeks.
What does this support? Grabbing and oral exploration
Materials: Wooden pearls, baby wool, bells

When? From 6 weeks.
What does this support? Grabbing, arm muscles, self-efficacy

RATTLES

As soon as your baby can grasp objects, you can offer them their first rattle. The rule here is: less is more. Choose rattles made of natural materials with appealing sounds and a pleasant feel, rather than many different rattles made of plastic. Wooden rattles are particularly suitable for the first months of life. Once your baby is a bit bigger and has mastered grasping better, you can offer them different rattles you have made yourself that make different sounds. You will find instructions in the chapter with play ideas for babies from 6 months of age.

O-BALL

O-balls are very popular with babies because they are particularly easy to grip and usually have bright colors. Some o-balls even come with small, inserted rattling beads depending on your preference.

You can give the o-ball to your child to hold. Alternatively, you can attach the ball to the playing arch to change things up a bit. Your child will try to grab it. If the child succeeds, they will probably pull on it enthusiastically. To prevent the playing arch from falling over, you can tie or sew a rubber band to the string with which you attach the ball so that your child can actually pull the ball down towards them. This strengthens hand-eye coordination and, at the same time, promotes strength in the hands.

When? From 7 weeks.
What does this support? Conscious grasping and letting go

SOFT BUILDING BLOCKS

When? From 10 weeks.
What does this support? Conscious grasping, perception of bodies, playing in the prone position

Building blocks do not necessarily have to be made of wood. Stacking blocks, in particular, are often made of plastic. Your child can feel them with interest and safely explore them with their mouth. You can also offer the building blocks to your child while they are lying on their stomach. Supporting the child with a rolled blanket or towel underneath the chest may be a good idea.

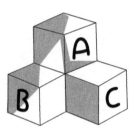

EXERCISES FOR EVERY DAY

IMITATE FACIAL EXPRESSIONS

Sit down comfortably and place your child on your angled legs. Chat with them, using different facial expressions. You will be surprised how your child tries to imitate your facial expression. This becomes particularly interesting once your child is two months old.

SPEAK ABOUT EVERYDAY THINGS

Babies are completely dependent on their parents. They have their diapers changed or are held, and their clothes changed, picked up, and carried around. To make it more comfortable and less abrupt for your baby, gently move them and refrain from sudden and jerky movements. Tell your child what you are going to do. For example, announce that you are now going to pick them up. Also, when changing and dressing, say what you are doing.

PUT UP A MIRROR

Place a low, wide mirror on the wall beside the playing arch. This way, your child can look at the mobiles from different perspectives. For example, you can find shatterproof versions at low prices in inexpensive furniture store chains.

If your child prefers to turn its head to one side only, you can place the mirror on the less popular side and encourage the child to turn in that direction. This helps to prevent tension or a crooked posture.

However, you can also use the mirror without a playing arch, for example, when your child is lying on their stomach. They are sure to find their own reflection very interesting.

FREE HANDS

Parents often stick their infant's hands into gloves made of light cotton. These are supposed to ensure the children do not scratch and injure themselves with their fingernails. In Montessori education, such gloves are deliberately not used. Babies should experience their environment with all their senses and develop a good understanding of their bodies. Moreover, even unborn babies calm themselves in the womb with their hands. This calming strategy should not be artificially prevented, especially in the early period after birth. Later, their hands will be the first things the child consciously explores with its mouth.

33

THREE TO SIX MONTHS

Motor development: The grasping reflex of three-month-old babies decreases more and more and is now replaced by purposeful grasping. At first, it is still difficult for your child to let go of objects. But by the age of six months, the grasping reflex has completely disappeared, and objects can be released, turned in the hands, turned around, thrown, and even shaken at will. Offer your child grasping toys that motivate them to explore carefully and be placed from one hand to another.

Babies can now hold their heads securely and control their torsos. They are becoming increasingly mobile, turning from their tummy to their back and later in the opposite direction. Many children make their first attempts to crawl, and some can already move a few centimeters forward.

Sensory development: Your child explores different textures extensively, preferably with the mouth. This is called the oral phase. Your child can see spatially, recognize things a little further away, and follow them with eyes. You can now offer your child mobiles in bright colors, for which they need more concentration.

Your baby can locate sounds and recognize the voices of their closest relatives. They turn to sources of sound. You can accommodate this development by offering your child different sound sources..

Language development: Your child begins to produce sounds and to babble the first syllables. They try to imitate the sounds they hear. Talk a lot with your child.

Cognitive and relational development: Your child smiles spontaneously at people and plays a lot. After being exclusively influenced by the closest people in the first months of life, your child is slowly developing a curiosity for other things. Children now begin to play extensively. Let your child discover their surroundings in peace, and do not disturb them when they are intensively playing. Do not comment on any actions during these phases but observe your child as they engage with their environment.

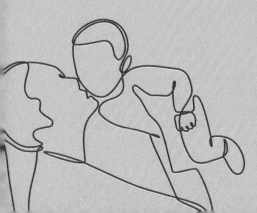

HAND·EYE·COORDINATION

GRABBING RINGS ON THE PLAYING ARCH

When? 3 Months and up
Time needed: 5 minutes
Preparation: Easy
What does this support? Purposeful grasping and letting go
Materials: Rings made of wood or plastic, ribbon, rubber band

Attach rings made of wood or plastic to the playing arch with a ribbon. Your child will try to reach for them; if they succeed, they will pull on them. So that the play arch does not tip over, you should also sew or tie a rubber band to it.

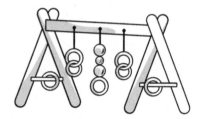

A PUZZLE BALL

The puzzle ball is a textile ball with a diameter of about 12.5 cm that has a little bell hidden inside and is sometimes also found under the name Takane Ball. You can crochet or sew this ball yourself. Free instructions for this can be found in abundance on the Internet.

These balls are easy to hold because of their special shape, and your child can easily pick up their puzzle ball with both hands and feet. Later, when your baby becomes more mobile, the puzzle ball offers incentives to slide on their bellies and crawl as the ball rolls.

When? 3 Months and up
Time needed: 2 hours or more
Preparation: Easy
What does this support? Purposeful grasping, hand-hand-coordination
Materials: Little bells, fabric for crocheting or sewing

SAVING TOYS

When? 4 Months and up
Time needed:
5 Minutes
Preparation: Easy
What does this support?
Hand-eye coordination,
hand muscles
Materials: Grabbing toys,
masking tape

Attach grasping toys your
child knows to the floor with
masking tape and let your
child pull them off the floor.

PULLING SILKEN CLOTH OR TISSUES OUT OF A BOX

Place a cardboard box with tissues in front of your child
and let your child pull out the tissues. Hold the box
while doing this so your child can fully concentrate on
pulling them out. Of course, you can still use the tissues
afterward.

If your child immediately puts the tissues in their mouth,
you can alternatively put silk cloths knotted together
into the box. This game idea is also fun for older babies
who can sit alone and hold the box without help.

When? 4 Months and
up
Time needed:
5 Minutes
Preparation: Easy
**What does this
support?** Purposeful
grasping and letting go
Materials: Cardboard
box, tissues, or silk cloths

INTERLOCKING DISCS

When? 5 Months and
up
**What does this
support?** Putting things
from one hand into the
other

Interlocking discs are a very simple yet effective
wooden toy consisting of two discs attached to
each other, each 5 cm in diameter. They are
particularly suitable for exploring with both
hands. If the disc should ever fall, it does not
roll far away, so your child can simply pick it up
alone and is not unnecessarily frustrated.

FORMS AND COLORS

PUTTING UP BOOKS IN A SEMICIRCLE

Place open books in a semicircle. Place your child in the middle and let them look at the books. Make sure that only one picture is shown on each page. At first, books contrasting the baby's early days are suitable. Still, later, you can also use clearly drawn coloring pages.

When? 3 Months and up
Time needed: 5 Minutes
Preparation: Easy
What does this support? Perception of contrasts, concentration, torso control
Materials: Contrast books

THE DANCER MOBILE

The dancer mobile is only suitable for older babies aged about 3 months and over because it imitates the dynamic movement of a human being and demands a fair amount of concentration from your child. The three parts that make up each dancer move independently of each other.

You can make the dancers out of hologram foil or metallic colored construction paper, for example, so that they shine beautifully and are additionally interesting for your child. A dancer's head consists of a circle, and the arms and legs each have the shape of a stylized crescent. When you join the individual parts with a needle and thread, make sure you leave a little space between the individual components so that the mobile looks as dynamic as possible.

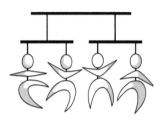

When? 3 Months and up
Time needed: An hour
Preparation: Medium
What does this support? Spatial vision, concentration
Materials: Hologram foil, colored construction paper, needle, thread

RAINBOW COLORS ON THE PLAYING ARCH

Hang colored rings on ribbons from the same color scheme on the playing arch. Your child will be fascinated by the strong contrasts of the colors.

When? 3 Months and up
Time needed: 5 Minutes
Preparation: Easy
What does this support? Perception of primary colors, concentration
Materials: Colored rings, ribbons

BALLS IN DIFFERENT SIZES

When? 3 Months and up
What does this support? Perception of size

Offer plain balls in different colors to your child in the prone position. These balls can be made of wood or felt, but you can also crochet or sew them. Each ball should be a different size.

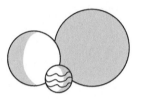

A SIMPLE GAME OF SHADOWS

This game idea is very easy to implement with household materials. Stretch cling film over one of the two empty toilet paper roll openings, then put a rubber band on the cling wrap to secure it. Using colored markers or paint, draw a simple shape onto the film, such as a star or a heart. Darken the room and shine a flashlight in the free opening of the toilet paper roll. This will allow you to project the drawn shape onto the wall. Take your baby into your arms and move away from the wall and back towards it so that the shadow image changes size.

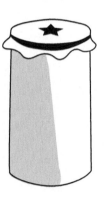

When? 4 Months and up
Time needed: 15 Minutes
Preparation: Easy
What does this support? Vision, attention, concentration
Materials: Cling film, empty toilet paper roll, rubber, pencil, flashlight

LANGUAGE AND LISTENING

PUZZLE BALL ON THE PLAYING ARCH

When? 3 Months and up
Time needed: 5 Minutes
Preparation: Easy
What does this support? Concentration, perception of sounds
Materials: Puzzle ball

Hang the puzzle ball on the playing arch so your child can touch it but not grasp it firmly. The little bell in the ball encourages your child to kick the puzzle ball with their legs or hit it with their hands.

OVEN BAG

Babies love everything that crackles. And an oven bag can do that particularly well. Cut a strip off and put something interesting in it, for example, small colored pompoms. Tie the bag at both ends like a Christmas cracker so nothing falls out. Your child will be thrilled to feel the tube, enjoy the crackling sound and explore the contents. Never leave your child unattended, as there is a risk of suffocation with any type of bag which could be pulled on their face.

When? 3 Months and up
Time needed: 15 Minutes
Preparation: Easy
What does this support? Self-efficacy, touching, hearing
Materials: Oven bag, pompoms

When? 3 Months and up
Time needed: 15 minutes
Preparation: Medium
What does this support? Following moving objects with the eyes
Materials: Gloves, bells

GLOVE WITH BELLS

Sew little bells onto the fingertips of white or black gloves. Sing to your child or make little rhyming games and support them with the bells.

VARIOUS RATTLES

You can easily make rattles for your child yourself. Both opaque and transparent cans are suitable for this. For example, you can use small film canisters or glue the canister of vitamin tablets with black and white construction paper and turn it into a monochrome rattle. Small containers that once contained breast milk or pre-nutrition pumped out in the maternity hospital, for example, are also suitable for this purpose. You can use rice, small or large beads, or sand for the contents. You can seal the tins with hot glue so your child cannot accidentally open them.

When? 3 Months and up
Time needed: 20 Minutes
Preparation: Easy
What does this support? Hearing, movement, muscles
Materials: Cans, construction paper, rice, sand, pearls, hot glue

41

KICKING A BAKING SHEET

When? 3 Months and up
Time needed: 5 Minutes
Preparation: Easy
What does this support? Hearing, movement
Materials: Baking sheet

Lay your child on the floor on their back and hold a baking sheet to their feet. As soon as your child kicks the baking sheet with their feet, they hear the muffled sound and will soon be kicking enthusiastically.

XYLOPHONE

A xylophone is suitable to use when your child can lie on their stomach, hold their head for a long time, and become quite confident in grasping. Your child will enjoy the different sounds of the instrument and get a feeling for the cause and effect of the sound. Older children also enjoy a xylophone, so this is a worthwhile investment.

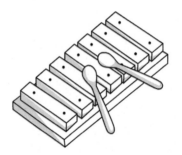

When? 5 Months and up
What does this support? Hearing, self-efficacy

LANGUAGE AND LISTENING

TOUCH

WATER PLAYING MATS

Water play mats are fascinating for babies. You can easily make these mats yourself and vary them again and again. The basis is a zip freezer bag. Fill it with water (a dash of baby oil also makes for interesting flow properties). Now you can fill the freezer bag with anything you like: Glitter, beads, food coloring, small decorative stars, etc. There are no limits to your imagination. However, these items should not have sharp edges so the bag is not damaged and allow the contents to leak out. You can attach the play mat to the floor with adhesive tape to prevent it from slipping and place your child in a prone position in front of it.

A similar activity can be done with sensory bottles. You can find a detailed description in the chapter with play ideas for children 6 months and older.

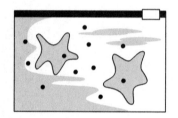

When? 3 Months and up
Time needed: 20 Minutes
Preparation: Medium
What does this support? Concentration, torso muscles
Materials: Zip freezer bag or bottle, water, baby oil, glitter, beads, food coloring

When? 3 Months and up
Time needed: 10 Minutes
Preparation: Easy
What does this support? Sensory perception with the feet
Materials: Tub, water, lentils, sand

SENSORY TUB FOR THE FEET

Babies don't just explore the world with their hands but also with their feet. Fill a shallow tub with interesting textured materials, and hold your baby so that their feet are in the tub. You can use warm water for this, lentils, sand, and even warm cooked spaghetti.

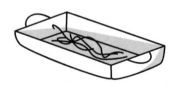

44

FEELING BAG

You can sew different feeling bags for your child. Fill them with cherry stones, lentils, grains like spelt (wheat), or rice. Don't make the bags too full so they don't break, even if they are touched enthusiastically. It's best to double-sew the edges so that nothing can fall out. Your child will enjoy these little bags for a long time. Later, they are also ideal for throwing and crawling after.

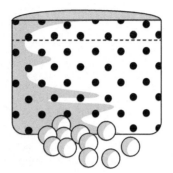

When? 4 Months and up
Time needed: 30 Minutes
Preparation: Medium
What does this support? Touching
Materials: Small bag, cherry stones, lentils, rice, or similar

When? 4 Months and up
Time needed: 5 Minutes
Preparation: Easy
What does this support? Torso and finger muscles
Materials: Tub, water, shower sponge, rings

WATER PLAYING TUB

Water games are popular even with the youngest of children. Place your child on their stomach in front of a baking sheet or a shallow tub filled with an inch (2,5 cm) of water. You can put a shower sponge, small painting sponges from craft supplies, or the rings of a buggy chain in the tub. There are no limits to your imagination. Please never let your child out of your sight during this activity. As with all water games, special care is needed here.

BUBBLE WRAP

Young and old children love bubble wrap. If you have colored Lego sheets in your household, you can cut the bubble wrap so that its edge length is about 10 cm longer than one of these Lego sheets and use it as a colored base. Attach both to the floor with tape and let your child feel the bumpy surface. If you do not have any Lego sheets, you can paint a piece of cardboard and place it under the bubble wrap.

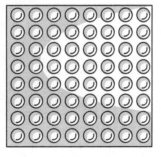

When? 5 Months and up
Time needed: 15 Minutes
Preparation: Easy
What does this support? Fine motor skills
Materials: Bubble wrap, Lego sheets or cardboard, adhesive tape

TOUCH

SIX TO NINE MONTHS

~

Motor development: Your baby's motor skills are developing rapidly, and the infant is becoming increasingly mobile. The child learns to sit by themselves and begins to roll, belly crawl, and crawl on all fours. Some children can already pull themselves up to a standing position at nine months. You can support your child in these important developmental steps by offering play activities that motivate movement.

Your baby can grasp objects with both hands and safely transfer them from one hand to the other. They are now slowly exploring objects with their hands rather than their mouths first. Your child will enjoy exploring gravity and dropping things repeatedly. Offer your child toys with exciting textures and balls to throw.

The painting development of children can be divided into seven phases. The first of these is finger painting. The child handles mushy or liquid substances such as water, sand, mud, or snow and "paints" with them through their movements. The child repeats this for the fun of the movement and to leave even more traces. This painting process's result is irrelevant; it is only about the process itself. You can encourage this phase by offering your child appropriate textures to paint with.

Sensory development: Your child's field of vision is continuously expanding, and they can now see things sharply outside their range. Objects are no longer explored exclusively with the mouth and hands but also with the eyes. They show increasing interest in their surroundings.

Language development: Your child begins to babble and forms first-syllable chains. Some children already say their first word during this period. Children develop a broader passive vocabulary during this time. Read to your child regularly. This will ensure a continuous expansion of their vocabulary.

Cognitive and relational development: During this period, your child begins to communicate and play with you using sounds and facial expressions. They recognize that they have a permanent place within the family.

Cognitively, your child makes a giant developmental leap. They now understand that people and objects outside their perception still exist. Your child now understands that someone who leaves the room will soon return. This is called object permanence. You can foster this understanding in your baby through games where toys seem to disappear and reappear in drawers or other places they explore.

HAND·EYE·COORDINATION

PULLING POMPOMS OFF A LINT ROLLER

This exercise can be done in the prone position and later while sitting freely. Simply stick a few colored pompoms on a lint roller and give the object to your child. Show them how you pull a pompom off the roll in a slow movement. Your baby will now pull the pompoms off as well.

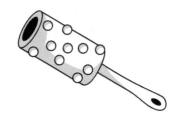

When? 6 Months and up
Time needed: 5 Minutes
Preparation: Easy
What does this support? Hand-eye-coordination, finger muscles, pincer grip
Materials: Pompoms, lint roller

When? 6 Months and up
Time needed: 10 Minutes
Preparation: Easy
What does this support? Fine motor skills, arm muscles
Materials: Pipe cleaners, pasta strainer

PIPE CLEANER IN A PASTA STRAINER

Put the pipe cleaner into a pasta strainer and let your child pull it out. This exercise is best done when your child has developed the ability to sit unsupported. Still, it is also possible to do it in a prone position.

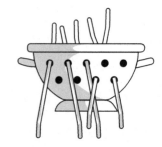

PULLING POST-IT NOTES OFF

Stick colored Post-it notes on a floor-to-ceiling windowpane or a mirror, and let your child peel them off. Vertical play makes a fundamental change in daily life.

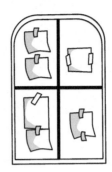

When? 7 Months and up
Time needed: 5 Minutes
Preparation: Easy
What does this support? Fine motor skills, arm and shoulder muscles
Materials: Post-it notes, mirror

THE FIRST STACKING TOWER

When? 7 Months and up
What does this support? Fine motor skills

You can now offer your child their first stacking tower. Large rings are ideal for this, as their large diameter makes them particularly easy to put on and take off. You can also use a ring and a kitchen roll holder. Offer your child only one ring at first and increase the number over time. Initially, your child will probably pull off the ring and then put it directly into their mouth.

PUSHING JAR LIDS THROUGH A SLIT IN A BOX

Cover a cardboard box or a tissue box with colored paper. Cut a wide slit in the top. Offer your child this box together with a basket of jar lids. Demonstrate the exercise slowly to your child and put a lid through the slit.

When? 8 Months and up
Time needed: 20 Minutes
Preparation: Medium
What does this support? Fine motor skills
Materials: Cardboard, colored paper, scissors, basket with jar lids

When? 8 Months and up

Time needed: 20 Minutes

Preparation: Medium

What does this support? Fine motor skills

Materials: Two shoe boxes, scissors, hot glue gun, basket

BALL THROWING BOX

Cut a circular hole in the bottom of an old shoebox. Take the lid of a larger cardboard box and glue the shoebox to the inside of the lid with a hot glue gun so that the hole is at the top. Your child can now throw balls into the top of the box (offer them in a separate basket), and they will roll into the "runway" you made out of the big lid without moving too far away.

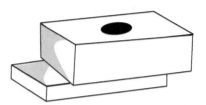

THE EGG PUZZLE

A wooden egg with a wooden egg cup is an excellent first puzzle for your child. Your child will enjoy putting the egg in and taking it out. This creates a direct connection to the child's environment.

When? 8 Months and up

What does this support? Fine motor skills

FORMS AND COLORS

SHADOW GAMES

When? 6 Months and up

What does this support? Attention, concentration, tracking moving objects with the eyes

We have already discussed a very simple shadow game for small babies. Darken the room and provide a light source; you can cast shadows against the wall with your hands. You can also give your child a flashlight and let them play with it. When your baby is half a year old, their ability to concentrate improves, and you can play normal shadow games with them.

DISCOVERY BASKET FOR VARIOUS COLORS

Put together a discovery basket with items in matching colors. For example, you can put a yellow cloth, a rubber duck, and a lemon in a basket for the color yellow.

When? 6 Months and up

Time needed: 10 Minutes

Preparation: Easy

What does this support? Color perception

Materials: Discovery basket, rubber duck, lemon, cloth

SENSORY BOTTLES

When? 6 Months and up

Time needed: 15 Minutes

Preparation: Easy

What does this support? Perception, concentration

Materials: Plastic bottle, water, baby oil, glitter

This exercise is related to the water play mats from the previous chapter. Fill a small transparent plastic bottle about two-thirds full of water. A dash of baby oil makes for interesting flow properties. You can now fill the sensory bottle with assorted craft items: pompoms, glitter, small decorative stones, etc.

BUILDING A TOWER OUT OF BUILDING BLOCKS

Build a tower of colored blocks with your child. Stack the blocks one by one on top of each other while naming their colors. It is most likely still too difficult for your child to participate. But your child will take great pleasure in knocking the tower over afterward.

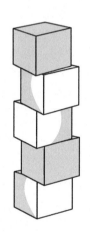

When? 8 Months and up

What does this support? Color perception

BOX WITH HOLES

When? 8 Months and up

Time needed: 15 Minutes

Preparation: Easy

What does this support? Perception of different heights

Materials: Shoebox, scissors, differently sized balls

Cut holes of different sizes in a shoebox. Offer your child different-sized balls to be put into the holes. Your child will notice that some openings are too small for some balls.

52

LANGUAGE AND LISTENING

RAINMAKER

A rainmaker imitates rain sounds and comes from Chilean culture. You can make a rainmaker yourself with some materials.

For this, you need the following:
- a tube of stacking crisps/chips or a shipping tube
- some nails
- baking paper
- rice or lentils
- 2 rubber bands
- masking tape
- material for decorating and sticking

Hammer the nails into the tube in a spiral. Cut out two pieces of baking paper. Place one piece of paper over one of the two openings and secure it with a rubber band. Now fill the tube to about a quarter with the rice or lentils. Close the second opening with the other sheet of baking paper and put on the second rubber band. Now, you can also wrap the tube with masking tape, so there is no risk of injury from the nails. Finally, you can decorate the tube with wrapping paper, glitter, etc., according to your preference. Flip the rainmaker upside down and back to show your child that sounds are made when the rainmaker is turned.

When? 6 Months and up
Time needed: 1 Hour
Preparation: difficult
What does this support? Hearing, gross motor skills
Materials: Tube, nails, baking paper, rice, rubber bands, masking tape, material for decoration

6 · 9 MONTHS

HITTING POT LIDS

When? 6 Months and up

Time needed: 5 Minutes

Preparation: Easy

What does this support? Hearing, gross motor skills, self-efficacy

Materials: Wooden spoon, several pot lids

Place or sit your child in front of a few pot lids and put a wooden spoon next to them. You can demonstrate to your child how to hit them with the spoon. Your child will find it very interesting to make these sounds independently.

MUSICAL INSTRUMENTS

You can offer your child their first musical instruments from the age of 6 months, for example, a small drum, two timbrels, and a bell. In the beginning, give your child only one musical instrument at a time so as not to overwhelm them. They will be busy enough discovering the shape and sound of the instrument. You can sing a song to your child and accompany them in playtime.

When? 6 Months and up

What does this support? Early musical education, hearing, self-efficacy

MUSIC BOX

When? 6 Months and up

What does this support? Fine motor skills, self-efficacy

Perhaps you already had a music box during pregnancy that you regularly played to your unborn child, or maybe a cuddly, musical toy is a fixed part of your child's bedtime ritual. Give your child the music box and demonstrate how to wind it up. Once your child succeeds in this movement, they will repeat it with pleasure. Of course, they will also extensively explore the music box or the cuddly toy with their mouth.

LISTENING CONTAINER

Your child becomes increasingly interested in different sounds at this age. You can fill opaque, easy-to-grasp containers (small film canisters) with different materials, such as sand, rice, lentils, a single wooden bead, a button, or a small bell. You can affix the lid with a hot glue gun. Offer your child several of these containers at one time so they can discover the different sounds one after the other.

When? 6 Months and up
Time needed: 20 Minutes
Preparation: Medium
What does this support? Hearing
Materials: Cans, rice, lentils or similar, hot glue gun

When? 6 Months and up
Time needed: 15 Minutes
Preparation: Easy
What does this support? Vocabulary
Materials: Laminated animal cards

CARDS WITH ANIMALS

You can show your child cards of different animals. It would be better if the cards were previously laminated. Name the animal and imitate the sound the animal makes. You can also name some details about the animal. So, for example: "This is a dog. It goes, 'Woof, woof!'. This dog is big and has brown fur." Avoid baby talk and phrases like, "This is a bow-wow doggy."

TOUCH

DRAWING WITH YOGURT

Since children at this age are still in the middle of the oral phase, using something edible for their first hand-painting activity is a good idea. Yogurt is particularly suitable and can be colored using food coloring. Sit your child in their highchair (sitting freely is a prerequisite) and use a spoon to place different colored amounts of yogurt at several points on the dining table or tray of the highchair. Your child does not need a demonstration of what to do; they will reach into the yogurt and begin the artistic process themselves.

When? 6 Months and up
Time needed: 5 Minutes
Preparation: Easy
What does this support? Drawing skills
Materials: Yogurt, food coloring, spoon

TOUCH

When? 6 Months and up
What does this support? Sense of touch
Materials: Hair curlers, basket

HAIR CURLERS

If you or your family members have hair curlers at home, you can offer them to your child in a small basket to explore. Your child will probably have had limited contact with spiky objects and find them particularly interesting.

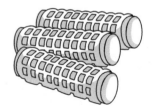

HULA-HOOP WITH SENSORY MATERIALS

Attach different objects with an interesting feel to a large hula-hoop. You can use cloth, some links of a buggy chain, tie a baby brush to a string, etc.

When? 6 Months and up
Time needed: 15 Minutes
Preparation: Medium
What does this support? Locomotion (circling), sense of touch
Materials: Hula hoop ring, cloths, or similar

SENSORY CUBE

Sensory cubes are suitable for children who can already sit independently and playtime in a prone position. A sensory cube is also well suited for traveling, such as a toy on car journeys. Buy a wooden cube with an edge length of approximately 6 cm at the hardware store. You can now glue the individual sides in different ways. You can use different fabrics (jeans, cotton, velvet), but also a piece of a bamboo mat, mirror foil, etc. Your child can turn this cube very well in their hands and pick it up directly if it should fall down because it does not roll far.

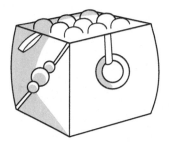

When? 6 Months and up
Time needed: 30 Minutes
Preparation: Medium
What does this support? Feeling
Materials: Wooden cube, various textiles, glue

SENSORY BALLS

Balls are a great joy for children who are already mobile, as they can crawl after them. Sensory balls are made of synthetic material and have different textures. This makes them easy for your child to grasp, and at the same time, they have an interesting texture.

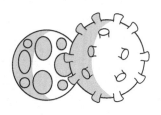

When? 6 Months and up
What does this support? Sense of touch, movement, throwing

DISCOVERY BASKET WITH SENSORY MATERIALS

When? 6 Months and up

Time needed: 5 Minutes

Preparation: Easy

What does this support? Your child learns about different haptics and expands their vocabulary.

Materials: Basket, baby brush, or other objects

The discovery baskets described previously can also be filled with sensory materials. For example, a baby brush, a comb, various sponges, or even a honey spoon are suitable.

SENSORY WALL

Think big! Similar to the sensory cube, which is also suitable for traveling, you can create an entire sensory wall for your child. This has the advantage of offering space for many different materials and encouraging your child to play vertically.

For a sensory wall, you need a few pieces of shipping boxes. Cut them to the same size and stick them together on the back with enough masking tape. Now you can assemble the sensory wall. You can use anything you can find around the house. The following items are suitable:

- various fabrics
- mirror foil
- large pompoms glued close together
- bubble wrap
- a grass mat
- dried spaghetti glued close together
- a piece of cork
- dried lentils glued close together like a carpet

Glue the individual objects in place with a hot glue gun and set up the sensory wall. Your child will develop an interest in it and explore it in depth.

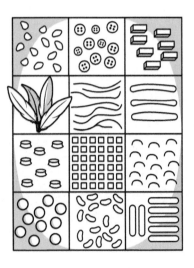

When? 6 Months and up

Time needed: 1 Hour

Preparation: Medium

What does this support? Sense of touch, arm muscles

Materials: Shipping box, scissors, masking tape, hot glue gun

THINKING TRAINING

PEEK-A-BOO

When? 6 Months and up
What does this support? Object permanence
Materials: Cloths

Hide your face behind a cloth and let your child pull it down. If your child is afraid to do this, you can use semi-transparent cloth at first. You can also put a light cloth over your child's head. However, if the child cannot pull the cloth down immediately, you should help so the child is not afraid.

PULLING CLOTHS OUT OF AN O-BALL

Pull cloths through an o-ball. Show your child how to pull out a cloth and then give the ball to your child. You can also use your child's socks instead of cloths. Make the exercise a bit trickier and tangle the cloths slightly. Your child should still be able to easily pull them out but will gain a sense of cause and effect.

When? 6 Months and up
Time needed: 5 Minutes
Preparation: Easy
What does this support? Fine motor skills, action planning
Materials: Cloths or socks, o-ball

PULLING BOX

When? 6 Months and up
Time needed: 15 Minutes
Preparation: Easy
What does this support? Sense of cause and effect
Materials: Opaque bottle, screwdriver, shoelaces

Clean an opaque bottle (for example, a drink or detergent bottle) very thoroughly. Poke an even number of holes in it with a screwdriver. Now you can pull a shoelace into the bottle through one hole and out through another. Tie a knot at both ends so the shoelace cannot be pulled out of the bottle completely. Repeat this until all the holes in the bottle have a shoelace through them.

Give your child the bottle and demonstrate pulling on a shoelace. Your child will imitate this and notice over time that tugging on one side will cause the shoelace to be pulled in on the other.

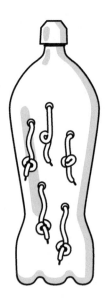

SAVING RUBBER DUCKS

Take a baking tin with a high rim and cover it crosswise with rubber bands. Place rubber ducks (or balls) at the bottom of the container and ask your child to free them from the baking tin.

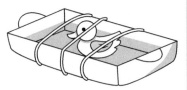

When? 6 Months and up
Time needed: 10 Minutes
Preparation: Easy
What does this support? Action planning, fine motor skills
Materials: Baking tin, rubber bands, rubber ducks

When? 6 Months and up
What does this support? Language development

BOOKS

There are appealing books with large, simple pictures and rhymes, even for very young children. Some are made of cardboard; others are tactile books.

THINKING TRAINING

NINE TO TWELVE MONTHS

~

Motor development: Your child can now sit down, pull up on furniture, or even stand up without assistance. Your child can walk a few steps while holding onto furniture or your hand. Many children take their first free steps during this period.

In these months, your child will train their pincer grip, i.e., grasping small objects with thumb and index finger. Playing activities with small things can also encourage your child to make this hand movement.

Sensory development: Your child can now identify objects even when they are only partially visible and is excellent at finding their way around their environment. Your baby turns to a sound to explore where it comes from.

Language development: Your child starts speaking their first words and understands simple sentences and instructions. You can expand your child's vocabulary by reading aloud and offering specific games. By pointing at objects and saying the name of it, your child's attention is drawn to the item.

Cognitive and relational development: Your child has fully developed its object permanence and knows that things that are not visible still exist. It has learned that objects have a center of gravity and that a tower can fall over. You can support your child's action by planning through appropriate play activities.

Your child expresses their emotional state through their voice. Your child's character becomes increasingly apparent. You can promote your child's autonomy by involving them in everyday tasks. Some of this can be done with crawling children. As soon as your child can walk freely, there are many more opportunities for active participation in everyday life.

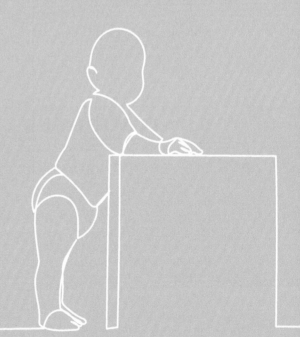

HAND·EYE· COORDINATION

WRAPPED TOYS

Wrap a new toy or one that has not been used for a while in tinfoil and let your child unwrap it. A more environmentally friendly alternative is wrapping paper or baking paper. However, tinfoil wraps around the toy better, making the exercise much more challenging. You can use it here if you have some left over. Do not leave your child unattended; otherwise, there is a risk of suffocation.

When? 9 Months and up
Time needed: 10 Minutes
Preparation: Easy
What does this support? Fine motor skills
Materials: Toys, tinfoil

HOUSEHOLD RUBBER BANDS ON TOILET ROLLS

Take an empty toilet roll and stretch household rubber bands on it. Demonstrate to your child how to pull a rubber band off the roll, then give them the roll, so they can repeat this exercise.

When? 9 Months and up
Time needed: 5 Minutes
Preparation: Easy
What does this support? Fine motor skills
Materials: Toilet roll, household rubber bands

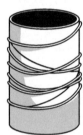

SOAP BUBBLES

Babies enjoy blowing soap bubbles. Sit your child on a blanket outside and blow bubbles in their direction. Your child will watch the bubbles bursting on their legs and arms and then try to touch them.

When? 9 Months and up
What does this support? Fine motor skills

STACKING PAPER CUPS

When? 9 Months and up
Time needed: 5 Minutes
Preparation: Easy
What does this support? Fine motor skills
Materials: Paper cups

Place three to five paper cups in front of your child and show them how you put one cup inside another. Your child will now try to imitate this exercise and repeatedly put the cups into each other and take them apart again.

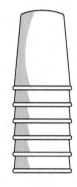

HUMMING TOP

A big humming top is great for babies. First of all, you can set the spinning top in motion. Your child will be fascinated by the movement and crawl after the top or stop it and explore it with their mouth first. Demonstrate the action again. In time, your child will try to spin the top by itself.

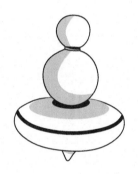

When? 9 Months and up
What does this support? Fine motor skills, movement

SORTING CHESTNUTS

When? 9 Months and up
Time needed: 15 Minutes
Preparation: Easy
What does this support? Fine motor skills
Materials: Chestnuts, basket, empty egg carton

This exercise is sure to bring a fall atmosphere into your living room. Collect chestnuts on a walk with your child and put a few in a basket at home. Offer your child an empty egg carton and slowly place a chestnut from the basket into the carton. Your child will imitate this movement. Stay with your child at all times. There is a risk of choking if your child puts a chestnut in their mouth.

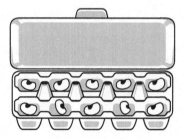

PULLING RINGS

If you have bought a Pikler triangle for your child, you can offer it to them from the age of 9 months to train their gross motor skills. But you can also do other things with it. Stick the double-sided tape on a large piece of cardboard and attach it to one side of the Pikler triangle or, if you don't have one, to a floor-to-ceiling window or door. Attach some rings to the tape. You can use the rings of a stacking game or the links of a buggy chain. Show your child how to pull one ring off the tape and let your child remove the other rings. This vertical play exercise trains your child's fine motor skills and arm muscles.

When? 9 Months and up
Time needed: 5 Minutes
Preparation: Easy
What does this support? Fine motor skills, arm and shoulder muscles
Materials: Pikler triangle, cardboard, adhesive tape, rings

HAND-EYE-COORDINATION

FORMS AND COLORS

When? 9 Months and up

Time needed: 5 Minutes

Preparation: Easy

What does this support? Movement

Materials: Toy tunnel or Pikler triangle, maybe colorful cloths

CRAWLING THROUGH A TUNNEL

Most babies love to crawl through colorful play tunnels. Due to the nature of the walls, their surroundings are bathed in colored light. If you don't have a play tunnel, you can use a Pikler triangle and drape it with colorful cloths.

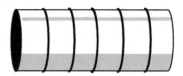

A FIRST PUZZLE

From the age of about 10 months, you can start offering your child puzzles. Puzzles with only one piece are best suited for this. These are available in typical Montessori shops, where you will usually find the three basic shapes circle, square, and triangle. At first, your child will explore the puzzle piece mainly with its mouth, but in time, they will try to take it out of the frame and put it back in again.

When? 9 Months and up

What does this support? Fine motor skills, engaging with shapes

When? 9 Months and up

Time needed: 5 Minutes

Preparation: Easy

What does this support? Fine motor skills, vocabulary

Materials: Sensory or felt balls, baskets, muffin tray

PLACING BALLS IN A MUFFIN TRAY

Offer sensory balls or different colored felt balls to your child in a basket with a muffin tray. Take a ball and place it in the muffin tray. Name the color of the ball. Your child will now try to move the other balls. Again, tell them what color the chosen ball is.

BOTTLES WITH NATURAL MATERIALS

Go for a walk with your baby and collect objects from nature. These can be flowers, moss, leaves, stones, and grass. Put the natural materials into bottles with a theme and seal them with a hot glue gun. Offer them to your child in a discovery basket, for example. Your child can now look at natural materials from all directions, and you don't have to be afraid that they might swallow something.

When? 9 Months and up
Time needed: 10 Minutes
Preparation: Easy
What does this support? Engaging with natural materials
Materials: Objects from nature, bottles, hot glue gun

When? 9 Months and up
Time needed: 10 Minutes
Preparation: Easy
What does this support? Fine motor skills
Materials: Shipping box, scissors, hot glue gun, squeeze pouch lid, or raw pasta

GETTING TO KNOW SHAPES

Cut two holes into the bottom of a shipping box. The holes should have two different shapes; a circle and a square are suitable to start with. Cut out some circles and squares from another piece of cardboard. The exercise aims for your child to sort them into the appropriate hole. To make it easier for your child to grasp, you can make a handle for the shapes by attaching a squeeze pouch lid or a raw noodle with a hot glue gun.

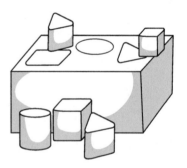

Alternatively, building block boxes with holes in the lid for the individual shapes or corresponding plug-in boxes are also suitable. However, the many different shapes may be too much for your child at this age, whereas with the self-made solution, you can add more and more shapes over time.

LANGUAGE AND LISTENING

LAMINATED FAMILY PICTURES

Print out pictures of family members and friends with whom your child regularly interacts. Round the corners and give the pictures to your child. Name the person depicted. This way, your child will learn the names of the people they regularly see.

You can also make a game out of it and attach the pictures to the wall. Stick a Post-it note over each person's face and let your child peel off the notes. Your child will enjoy seeing the familiar faces and, at the same time, internalize the names.

When? 9 Months and up
Time needed: 15 Minutes
Preparation: Easy
What does this support? Vocabulary
Materials: Pictures of family members, Post-it notes

MARBLE RUN

When? 9 Months and up
What does this support? Fine motor skills, hearing, self-efficacy

Babies who can sit safely enjoy the sounds of a marble run. Marble runs remain interesting even when the child is older because they are suitable for experiments: What slides faster? What makes the most noise? What happens when a few things go down at the same time? Marble runs are, therefore, a worthwhile investment. Ensure that the marbles are not too small; otherwise, there is a risk of choking. However, don't leave your child alone with larger balls, either. There are also marble runs with cars instead of marbles, which are less likely to be swallowed.

SURPRISE BOX

Cover a cardboard box with wrapping paper. Cut a circular hole at the top with a diameter of about 8 cm, so your child can comfortably put their hand and forearm into it. Disguise this hole with a few pieces of paper by cutting two sheets of paper about 10x8 cm and cutting them into 2 cm wide strips. Now glue the strips around the hole to create a fan curtain that covers the hole. You can now put fruit or vegetables in the box, preferably ones that can tolerate a little rough treatment, for example, an apple.

When? 9 Months and up
Time needed: 20 Minutes
Preparation: Medium
What does this support? Vocabulary
Materials: Cardboard, wrapping paper, scissors, paper, glue, fruit

Now, put your hand inside the box and pretend to look for something but do not find it. Shake the box so the objects make a noise, and offer it to your child. Your child will now try to unearth the box's contents and, in this way, internalize the name of the object found.

9 – 12 MONTHS

LANGUAGE AND LISTENING

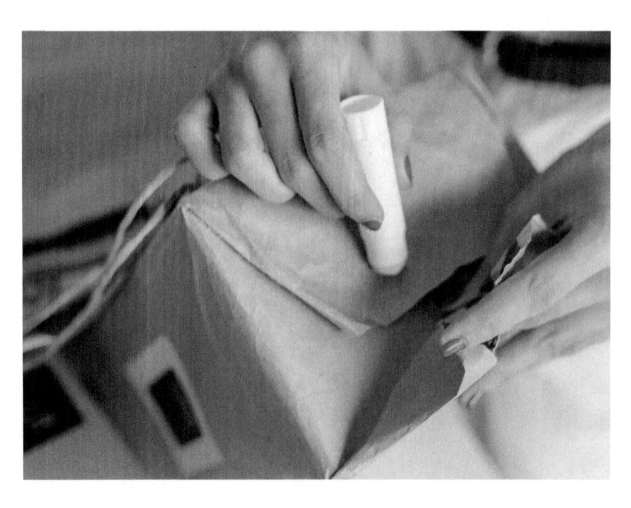

70

When? 9 Months and up
Time needed: 5 Minutes
Preparation: Easy
What does this support? Fine motor skills, self-efficacy

POP-ITS

Pop-Its are flat, colorful shapes with numerous round nubs the size of your thumb. These nubs can be pressed in with the fingers, which produces a popping sound. Pop-Its are often used with ADHD patients, but young children enjoy these toys. Babies are fascinated by the sounds made when pushed in and enjoy the self-efficacy they experience.

BOOKS

Your child is now at an age when you should read to them or look at books with them for at least 15 minutes a day. Your child will learn the language through the melody of the sound. For example, picture books with one animal per page or books with short rhymes are suitable for this.

You can give your child several books at once at this age (but there should not be more than five). Avoid placing the books on a bookshelf above the child's height, as is usual with adults. Your child cannot read yet, of course, and it helps them to recognize the book if they can see it from the front. Small book benches for children can be bought for this purpose. You can also screw a bookshelf to the wall. Spice racks, for example, are suitable for this purpose, out of which the books cannot fall and can stand with the cover facing the front.

When? 9 Months and up
Time needed: 15 Minutes
Preparation: Easy
What does this support? Vocabulary
Materials: Picture books

LANGUAGE AND LISTENING

TOUCH

When? 9 Months and up
Time needed: 5 Minutes
Preparation: Easy
What does this support? Taste
Materials: Tub, water, orange, lime, mint

WATER TUB WITH FOOD

Fill a shallow tub with an inch (ca. 2 cm) of water and place it in front of your child. Add orange slices, lime slices, and chopped mint one after the other. Change the water occasionally. Your child will examine the food in the water and almost certainly try it. In this way, several senses are addressed at once.

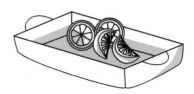

OOBLECK

An oobleck is a non-Newtonian fluid and an experience for young and older children. Non-Newtonian fluids become hard when pressure is applied to them. This is a new experience for your child as they work their hands through the mixture.

Mix corn flour and water in a bowl in a ratio of 2:1 and let your child experiment with the liquid. If you like, you can color the oobleck with food coloring beforehand. The oobleck is delightfully easy to dispose of: when it has hardened, you can simply suck it up with the vacuum, and when it is liquid, you can dilute it and pour it down the drain.

When? 9 Months and up
Time needed: 5 Minutes
Preparation: Easy
What does this support? Sense of touch, sense of physical properties
Materials: Corn flour, water, bowl, oobleck

COLORED ICE CUBES

When? 9 Months and up

Time needed: 5 Minutes

Preparation: Easy

What does this support? Sense of touch

Materials: Water, ice cube molds, food coloring, zip bags

Fill small ice cube molds with water, add a few squirts of food coloring to each, and freeze everything. Then offer the ice cubes to your child in a sealed zip bag. Your child can still experience the cold through the bag and also experience how the ice cubes liquefy into colored water.

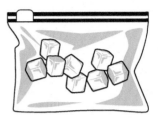

STONES IN A BATH

Fill a shallow tub with an inch (2,5 cm) of water and put a few larger stones in it. Your child can now throw these stones into the water to their heart's content and enjoy the splashing water. You can also refill the water occasionally if too much has already been splashed. This exercise is suitable for the balcony or the garden. Never leave your child unattended, as choking or drowning could occur.

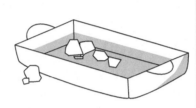

When? 9 Months and up

Time needed: 5 Minutes

Preparation: Easy

What does this support? Arm muscles, self-efficacy

Materials: Tub, water, stones

When? 9 Months and up

Time needed: 5 Minutes

Preparation: Easy

What does this support? Sense of touch

Materials: Ice cubes, sand

DIFFERENCES IN TEMPERATURE

You can introduce temperature differences to your child by putting ice cubes in one bowl and warm sand in another. Hold one of your child's hands in the bowl of ice, and say "cold," then hold the other hand in the bowl of sand and say "warm." Your child will indeed be fascinated by the differences in temperature.

THINKING TRAINING

PINK TOWER

The Pink Tower is a classic piece of Montessori equipment. It consists of 10 cubes, with the largest edge having a length of 10 cm. The edge length of each smaller cube is always 1 cm shorter than that of the previous one. The smallest cube, therefore, has an edge length of 1 cm. Unlike other stacking towers, the Pink Tower is not hollow but made of wood. Thus, the individual cubes differ in size, volume, and weight.

Place the second largest cube on top of the largest and show your child how to build a tower. This will probably not be easy for your child at first, but they will develop more and more skills over time. Handling the smallest cube also requires quite a lot of skill and trains the pincer grip.

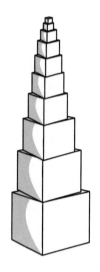

When? 9 Months and up
What does this support? Fine motor skills, sense of physical relationships, weight, and sizes

When? 9 Months and up
What does this support? Fine motor skills, logical thinking

BEAD MAZE

Offer your child a bead maze or a bead cube. Your child will enjoy moving the individual parts around and trying to figure out how best to do this.

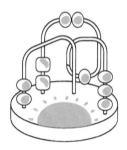

SMALL LOCK WITH A KEY

Children of this age love to put things some-
where and take them out again. This exercise is
a special cognitive and fine motor challenge. All
you need is a standard padlock. Tie the key to
the lock with a string and show your child how to
insert it into the lock and pull it out again. Your
child will now try to do the same. At first, they
will undoubtedly fail, but with time, they will get
better and better at it.

When? 9 Months and
up
Time needed:
15 Minutes
Preparation: Easy
**What does this
support?** Fine motor
skills, pincer grip,
logical thinking,
concentration
Materials: Padlock, key

IMBUCARE BOX

An Imbucare box is a small box made of wood
in which there is a hole at the top into which
a ball can be inserted. The ball falls down into
a small drawer that the child has to open to
retrieve the ball. This is meant to make it clear
to the child that the ball they just put in the
hole is still there, even if it is not visible at the
moment.

You can also build such a box yourself using a
cardboard box. As an alternative to the drawer, you can also cut a hole in the front of the
box through which your child can reach for the
ball. The opening should not be deep enough
for the ball to roll out independently.

When? 9 Months and
up
Time needed:
15 Minutes
Preparation: Easy
**What does this
support?** Object
permanence
Materials: Imbucare
box, ball

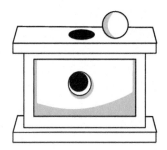

THINKING TRAINING

75

BUSY BOARD

On the one hand, a Busy Board is an elaborate DIY task requiring a little manual skill. Still, on the other hand, it is also something that will give your child pleasure far beyond their first birthday. Ready-made Busy Boards of an appealing size usually cost over $100 U.S. Hence, a homemade solution is well worth it financially.

For the DIY version, you need a wooden panel and various objects that are interesting for your child that you can attach to it. Suitable for this are, for example:

- various fasteners: Zip, safety chain
- light switch
- various locks with passive keys
- a bicycle bell
- interlocking, rotating gears
- a mirror
- wooden balls on a string (the string is tied at the back; the balls can be moved)
- large magnets
- castors (like those found under rolling boards)
- a socket with a plug
- a xylophone
- a plug-in puzzle in the shape of the child's name

When? 9 Months and up
Time needed: Multiple hours
Preparation: difficult
What does this support? Sense of touch, fine motor skills, logical thinking, attention, concentration

You can easily assemble a Busy Board from things you can find in your household. You can find more parts at the hardware store. Depending on the materials used, a self-made Busy Board should be around $30 to $40. The possibilities are endless.

THINKING TRAINING

When? 11 Months and up
Time needed: 15 Minutes
Preparation: Easy
What does this support? Fine motor skills, action planning, logical thinking
Materials: Various boxes and cases

OPENING AND CLOSING CONTAINERS

Around the first birthday and above, children love to open and close objects. You can offer your child different boxes and cartons and demonstrate how to open them. Your child will try to do this on their own. Change the objects regularly to keep the activity exciting for your child.

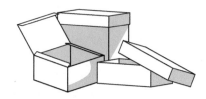

PRACTICAL LIFE EXERCISES

Practical life exercises usually begin at the dinner table for children not yet one year old. Your child learns to eat food with their fingers, swallow less and less, start drinking from a glass, and use a fork. As soon as your child can stand freely, you can also involve them in household tasks.

DRINKING FROM A SMALL CUP OR GLASS

You should already be offering your child liquids with their complementary food. If you have not yet done so, you should start offering your child water in a small glass or cup. For example, glasses your child can hold well or small espresso cups are suitable. If you have nicely shaped egg cups, your child can also drink from them.

When? 9 Months and up
What does this support? Fine motor skills
Materials: Small glasses or cups, water

When? 9 Months and up
What does this support? Fine motor skills

EATING SMALL PIECES

So far, you have offered your child either purée, finger food, or a combination of both. You should introduce your child to solid food no matter which forms you have started with complementary feeding. A good motor skill exercise is to have your child take small pieces (fruit or sugar-free round cornflakes) with a pincer grip.

SETTING THE TABLE

You can show your child how a table is set. There are silicone mats that have the outlines of plates, cutlery, and glasses drawn on them. However, you can also design a mat by drawing it on a large sheet of paper and placing it under a dirt-repellent, transparent mat. When doing this, you can ensure that the cutlery is not drawn next to the plate, as is classically the case, but above it. This has the advantage that your child can freely decide which hand to use to grasp the cutlery. In this way, they are not unconsciously forced into a certain handedness.

When? 9 Months and up
What does this support? Setting the table
Materials: Paper, pen, transparent pad

When? 10 Months and up
What does this support? Standing, self-efficacy

GETTING LAUNDRY FROM THE WASHING MACHINE

Doing the laundry is a big part of any family household, and there are different activities here that your child can do as they get older. Young children who can stand safely can pull the laundry out of the washing machine and throw it into the laundry basket. You can use the learning tower for help if your washing machine is elevated.

When? 11 Months and up
What does this support? Fine motor skills
Materials: Egg holder, eggs (either hard-boiled or made of wood)

SORTING EGGS

Let your child sort eggs into an egg holder from the fridge. You can use hard-boiled eggs or wooden play eggs for this. If you are very brave, try it out with raw eggs under supervision.

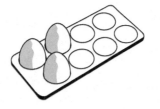

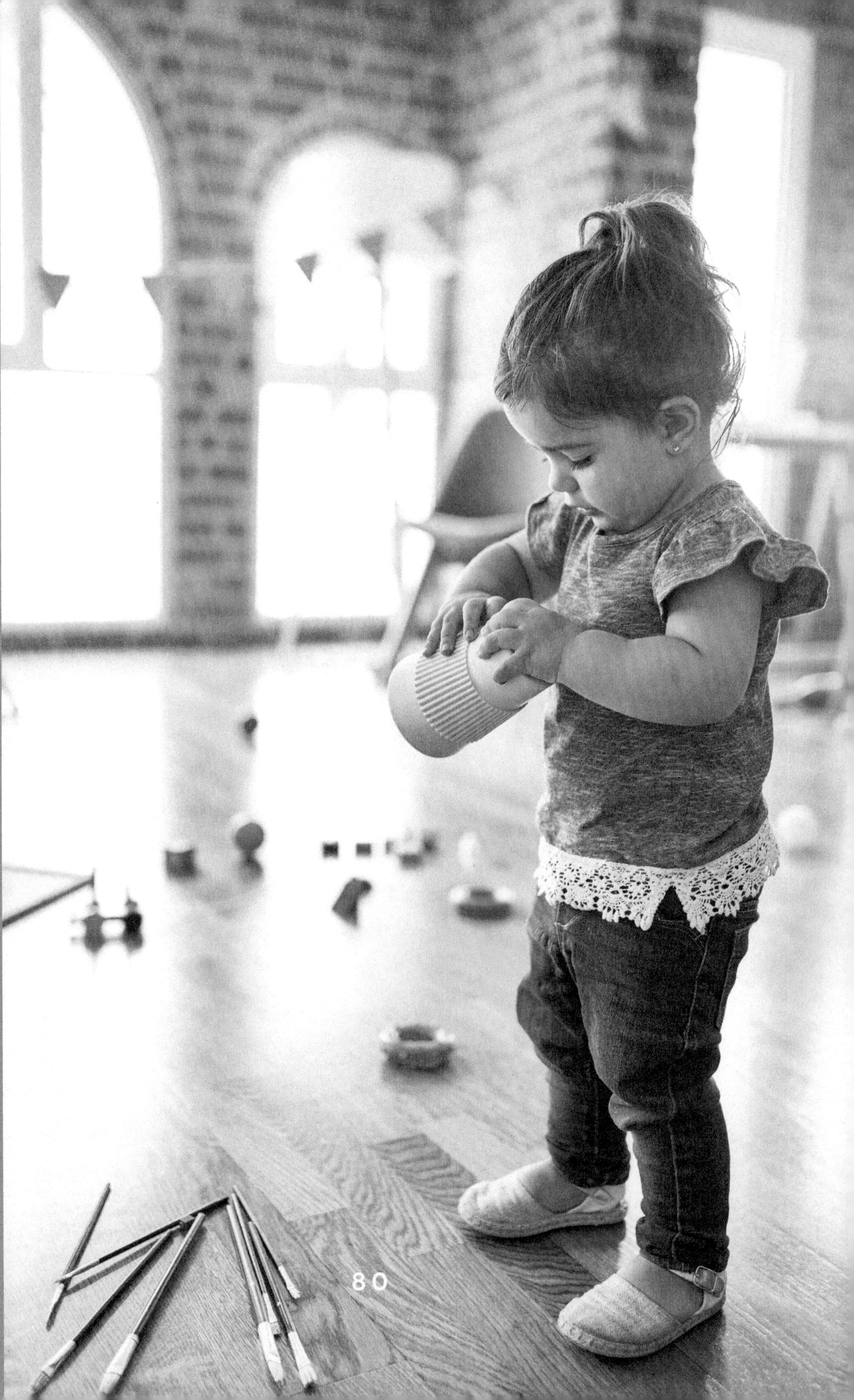

ONE YEAR TO ONE AND A HALF YEARS

~

Motor development: During this period, children learn to stand without holding on and to walk freely. They can bend or lean forward and stand up again, enjoy pulling objects with them, and try to lift heavy things. Many children enjoy climbing, and some already try hopping. At 18 months, most children can take a few steps backward and climb stairs on all fours.

At one and a half years, most children can eat alone with a fork and spoon, build a tower with three or four blocks and draw a line on paper.

Sensory development: Your child's distance vision is now fully developed, and their vision is comparable to an adult's. They can easily follow moving objects.

Language development: Your child can speak their first words and point to things (for example, body parts) when asked. They can combine words and gestures to express something. At 18 months, some children can already speak up to 50 words. Starting with this active vocabulary, the so-called vocabulary explosion occurs, and the number of actively spoken words increases rapidly.

Cognitive and relational development: Your child can imagine things and learn how to use everyday things like the telephone. Some children already sort toys by color, shape, or size. Your child takes toys apart and puts them back together again.

For many children, the autonomy phase begins now, previously usually called the "phase of defiance." Your child strives for independence in many areas, wants to eat and dress alone, for example, and will often be frustrated because they have not yet mastered many things. Your child will often say, "No!" and throw tantrums. Follow these calmly and mirror your child's feelings. Name their feelings with words and allow them to act them out. Comfort your child afterward and remain present the whole time. Offer comfort.

Your child enjoys being with other children and adults and is good at showing affection. They recognize their own reflection in the mirror and imitate other people.

1 - 1.5 YEARS

HAND·EYE·COORDINATION

PUTTING COTTON BALLS INTO AN EMPTY BOTTLE

On a tray, offer your child an empty, clear plastic bottle without a lid and cotton balls in a small separate container. Slide a cotton ball into the bottle and encourage your child to imitate it.

When? 1 year and up.
Time needed: 5 Minutes
Preparation: Easy
What does this support? Fine motor skills
Materials: Tray, plastic bottles, and cotton buds in a separate container

When? 1 year and up.
Time needed: 5 Minutes
Preparation: Easy
What does this support? Fine motor skills
Materials: Pompons, whisk, basket

GETTING POMPOMS OUT OF A WHISK

Put pompoms in a whisk and give the whisk to your child together with a small basket. Demonstrate to them how you pull a pompom out of the whisk and throw it into the basket. Your child will repeat this action.

PULLING WASHI TAPE OFF THE WALL

Stick washi tape in appealing colors on the wall. Show your child how to remove the tape and leave the rest of the tape to them. To make the exercise a little easier, leave a small corner sticking out at the end so your child can pull the tape off easily with the pincer grip.

When? 1 year and up.
Time needed: 5 Minutes
Preparation: Easy
What does this support? Fine motor skills, pincer grip, arm and shoulder muscles
Materials: Washi tape

When? 1 year and up.
Time needed: 5 Minutes
Preparation: Easy
What does this support? Fine motor skills, sense of touch, concentration, attention
Materials: Tub, lentils or rice, spoons

POURING EXERCISES

Fill a shallow tub with dried lentils or rice. Offer your child various utensils for pouring games in this action tub, for example, spoons, ladles, funnels, or scoops. Your child will be attracted to play with these sensory materials in the action tub.

INSERTING COINS

Place a piggy bank or cash box on a tray with a small container of coins. Show your child how to put a coin into the piggy bank or cash box, and invite your child to try it too. The ringing of the coins as they fall in will further motivate your child.

When? 1 year and up.
Time needed: 5 Minutes
Preparation: Easy
What does this support? Fine motor skills, concentration
Materials: Piggy bank, tray, coins

STICKING SNOW ON A SNOWMAN

When? 1 year and up.
Time needed:
5 Minutes
Preparation: Easy
**What does this
support?** Fine motor
skills
Materials: Dark paper,
white pencil, glue
stick, container, white
pompoms

Draw a snowman on a dark sheet of paper with a white pencil and coat the surface of the snowman with a glue stick. Offer your child the prepared paper with a small container filled with white pompoms. Stick a pompom on the tacky surface and explain to your child that they will now cover the snowman with snow. Encourage your child to do the activity.

This exercise is perfect during the cold season. Pre-paint an ice cream cone with several layers on top in the summertime. Then, stick different colored pompoms on it to represent different flavors of ice cream. In the fall, you could alternatively use a pumpkin and orange pompoms.

THROWING A BALL AGAINST THE WALL

When? 15 months and
up.
Time needed:
10 Minutes
Preparation: Easy
**What does this
support?** Throwing
movement, aiming
ability, arm and
shoulder muscles
Materials: Masking
tape, tinfoil, a soft or
squishy ball

Using masking tape, tape an approximately 25 x 25 cm piece of tinfoil to the wall or door. This is a target area. Encourage your child to hit this target with a soft ball when throwing it. The foil crackling will tell you both when the target has been hit.

HAND-EYE-COORDINATION

FORMS AND COLORS

SORTING CIRCLES BY COLOR

When? 1 year and up.
Time needed:
10 Minutes
Preparation: Easy
What does this support? Understanding of colors, first sorting exercise
Materials: Cardboard paper, scissors, paper, tray, basket

Cut out approximately 20 circles from cardboard or construction paper in two different colors. These do not have to be the same size. Take a white sheet and glue half the colored circles onto it using both colors while keeping them separate. Offer the sheet to your child on a tray and put the circles in a basket on the tray as well. Take a circle and place it on the sheet with the corresponding color. Repeat the action with a circle of the other color naming the colors as you do so. Encourage your child to copy this exercise. Once your child has become confident, you can add another color.

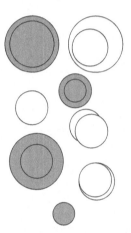

CREATING A DRAWING WALL

Your child is now moving from the finger-painting phase into the so-called scribbling phase. Now is the time to offer your child their first crayons, for instance, thick colored pencils or wax crayons that your child can hold easily in their hand. You can create a coloring wall for your child to express themselves artistically. Attach suitable paper rolls to the wall and allow your child to draw on the wall. Before this, however, you should explain to your child that drawing is only allowed on paper.

When? 1 year and up.
Time needed:
15 Minutes
Preparation: Easy
What does this support? Creativity
Materials: Pencils, paper

85

FORM PUZZLE

When? 15 months and up.
Time needed: 30 Minutes
Preparation: Medium
What does this support? Fine motor skills, understanding of shapes
Materials: Shipping box, scissors, glue, hot glue gun, squeeze pouch lid

To prepare this, you need two pieces of a shipping box of the same size (approximately 30x30 cm). Cut out various geometric shapes from one of these pieces (for example, a square, a triangle, a circle, a heart, a star, etc.) Now glue the second piece of cardboard onto the back of the first so that your puzzle has a back. You can glue the squeeze pouch lids on with a hot glue gun to add a handle to the shaped pieces. Offer your child the puzzle pieces in a basket that you place on top of the puzzle. Show them how to "puzzle" a piece correctly and encourage them to do the same.

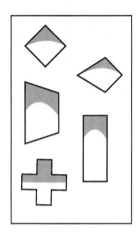

ICE BAG WITH COLORFUL CIRCLES

Draw a stylized ice cream cone on a sheet of paper. A light brown triangle represents the cone, and circles arranged on top of each other represent the individual scoops. After doing this, you should have a plain cone with empty circles on top. Draw several such ice cream cones with circles on a sheet of paper. Now cut out circles using colored construction paper. The circles should be the same size as the ones you drew on top of the cones. Offer the circles in a separate basket. Place a circle on the ice cream cone to build the scoops. Ask your child to match the other circles as well. The inside of the cones can be painted to match the circles cut from the colored construction paper if preferred.

When? 15 months and up.
Time needed: 15 Minutes
Preparation: Easy
What does this support? Recognizing colors
Materials: Paper, pencils, scissors

SENDING POMPOMS THROUGH TOILET ROLLS

When? 15 months and up.
Time needed: 10 Minutes
Preparation: Easy
What does this support? Distinguishing colors
Materials: Empty toilet paper rolls, glue, construction paper colors, container, pompoms

Gather 4 or 5 empty toilet paper rolls. Wrap each one in a different color of construction paper and tape the rolls vertically next to each other on the wall about 10 cm above the floor. Place a small container under each roll to catch items that drop through the rolls and offer pompoms in the colors of the rolls in another bowl. Take a pompom and toss it into the roll with the matching color. When the pompoms go into the roll, they land in the container you placed under them. Your child should now match all the pompoms correctly.

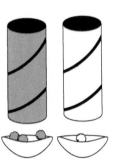

LANGUAGE AND LISTENING

LANGUAGE BASKET

Place toy animals in a small basket and offer them to your child to play with. While playing, you can always point out which animal is being played with and what sound it makes. Using animals that your child has already encountered daily is a good idea. They already have an inner image of these animals and a better connection to them.

When? 1 year and up.
Time needed: 5 Minutes
Preparation: Easy
What does this support? Vocabulary
Materials: Toy animals, basket

When? 1 year and up.
Time needed: 5 Minutes
Preparation: Easy
What does this support? Vocabulary
Materials: Laminated pictures of fruit and vegetables

ASSIGNING FOOD

Print out pictures of fruit and vegetables and laminate these cards. Put the cards on the dining table, together with the food pictured. Have your child match the food to the correct card.

HIDING ANIMAL FIGURES

Fill a shallow tub with dried lentils, chickpeas, or rice. Hide some of your child's animal figures in it. Show your child how to look for the figures and ask if they can find an animal too. Then ask them which animal it is or tell them yourself if your child cannot yet say the word.

When? 1 year and up.
Time needed: 5 Minutes
Preparation: Easy
What does this support? Vocabulary
Materials: Tub, lentils or similar, animal figures

MAKING A SMOOTHIE

Pick a smoothie recipe and put all the necessary ingredients on the table. Read one ingredient at a time to your child and ask your child to show you where that item is. You can then peel and prepare the ingredients letting your child help. Then have your child throw it into the blender. With this practical life exercise, your child can deepen their vocabulary at the same time. Always observe your child carefully around sharp objects and electricity.

When? 15 months and up.
Time needed: 5 Minutes
Preparation: Easy
What does this support? Vocabulary, self-efficacy
Materials: Ingredients for a smoothie

When? 15 months and up.
Time needed: 5 Minutes
Preparation: Easy
What does this support? Assignment of colors
Materials: Pencils, paper

COLOR HUNT

Draw a large circle onto a sheet of paper and divide it into 5 to 6 colors of your choice. Now point to a color and ask your child to look for something of the same color. Your child should now try to find other objects in the colors shown on their own or with you. If they do not succeed right away, you can help them and, for example, get a building block and place it on the circle's section that is the same color.

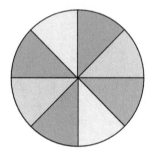

SINGING

Of course, you shouldn't wait until your child's first birthday to start singing to them. If your child can already speak a few words, you can sing songs to them that they are well acquainted with and pause before certain words and let your child complete them. You will be surprised how well your child can complete the verses.

When? 15 months and up.
What does this support? Vocabulary

LANGUAGE AND LISTENING

1 – 1.5 YEARS

TOUCH

NON-TOXIC PLAYING SLIME

When? 1 year and up.
Time needed:
15 Minutes
Preparation: Medium
What does this support? Sense of touch, hand muscles
Materials: Chia seeds, water, food coloring, tub, spoon, ladle

For this non-toxic playing slime, you will need the following:

- 25 g chia seeds
- 150 to 200 ml water
- some food coloring

Mix the chia seeds with water and food coloring. As it takes a few hours for the seeds to soak completely, it is a good idea to cover them and put them in the fridge overnight. The next day, a sticky slime will have formed. Now work (stir or use your hands) the mixture until you achieve the desired consistency, and the slime no longer leaves any stains. Offer the slime to your child to play with in an action tub with some utensils such as a spoon, fork, funnel, and ladle.

DIY SNOW

You can make snow at home, even during the summer or snowless winters. All you need is corn flour, baby oil, and, if you prefer, a little glitter. Mix the corn flour and the baby oil at a ratio of 8:1. You will hear it crunch nicely. Now pour the "snow" into a shallow tub or baking sheet. Offer some containers or toys for this, and let your child experiment with it as they like. If something lands on the floor, you can easily vacuum it up afterward.

When? 1 year and up.
Time needed:
5 Minutes
Preparation: Easy
What does this support? Sense of touch, fine motor skills
Materials: Corn flour, baby oil, tub, vessels, toys

TOUCH

89

PAINTING ICE

When? 1 year and up.
Time needed:
5 Minutes
Preparation: Easy
What does this support? Sense of touch, painting with brushes
Materials: Freezing tins, water, watercolors

Fill a large freezer container with two inches (ca. 5 cm) of water and place it in the freezer overnight. The next day, you can paint the block of ice with your child using watercolors. This exercise is especially suitable for hot summer days.

PLAYING FOAM

For this playing foam, mix the following ingredients together in a blender:

- 100 ml water
- 2 tbsp washing-up liquid
- 1 tbsp fine flour
- optionally a few drops of food coloring

Offer your child the foam in a tub. You can use toy figures with it. Note that the foam will collapse after some time, so do not prepare it too far in advance. Because of the soap included in this recipe, children should not consume the foam.

When? 1 year and up.
Time needed:
5 Minutes
Preparation: Easy
What does this support? Sense of touch
Materials: Water, washing-up liquid, flour, possibly food coloring, tub, play figures

When? 1 year and up.
Time needed:
5 Minutes
Preparation: Easy
What does this support? Creativity, hand muscles
Materials: Flour, salt, citric acid, water, cooking oil, food coloring, cookie cutters

MODELING CLAY

Mix the following ingredients in a blender:

- 400 g flour
- 200 g salt
- 2 tbsp citric acid
- 500 ml boiling water
- 3 tbsp cooking oil
- food coloring

Offer your child the modeling clay with some cookie cutters, then shape figures together.

THINKING TRAINING

PUZZLES

You can now offer your child puzzles with several pieces. Wooden jigsaw puzzles with 5 pieces are suitable.

When? 1 year and up.
What does this support? Understanding of shapes, logical thinking, concentration

When? 1 year and up.
What does this support? Concentration, attentiveness, fine motor skills, language acquisition

BOOKS WITH FLAPS

Also, offer books with flaps that your child can open. This way, your child can discover a book independently.

RUSSIAN DOLLS

Putting Russian dolls together in the correct sequence requires your child to be able to estimate the sizes correctly. Show your child how to separate and put the individual dolls back together. Take everything apart again and ask your child to put the figures into each other. As this exercise can be tricky from a motor point of view, depending on the doll, you may want to help your child with this.

When? 15 months and up.
What does this support? Understanding of sizes, logical thinking

FINDING THE RIGHT LIDS

When? 15 months and up.
Time needed: 5 Minutes
Preparation: Easy
What does this support? Feeling for different shapes, attention
Materials: Container with lid, tray

Gather several different containers, for example, freezer cases and screw-top jars. Place the lids separately on a tray and ask your child to match the correct covers to the containers.

LARGE OR SMALL?

Cut out two circles of colored construction paper, one very large and one very small. Glue these two onto a sheet of paper. Now cut out more circles, alternating large and small ones. Put them in a separate container and place everything together on a tray. Take a circle and place it with the large or the small glued-on circle. Comment on your actions and describe whether the circle is big or small. Take another circle and ask your child if it is big or small and where to put it. Your child will soon do this exercise independently.

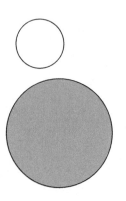

When? 15 months and up.
Time needed: 10 Minutes
Preparation: Easy
What does this support? Understanding of sizes
Materials: Scissors, colored construction paper, tray, container

PRACTICAL LIFE EXERCISES

When? 1 year and up.
Time needed:
5 Minutes
Preparation: Easy
What does this support? Fine motor skills, opening fastenings, autonomy, concentration
Materials: Pencil case, any object

OPENING A ZIP

Children at this age are very interested in fastenings. You can encourage this by offering your child a pencil case and putting a small object inside. This way, your child will learn to open and playfully close zips.

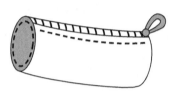

PEELING FRUIT

Engage your child in the kitchen and peel fruit together. A good choice is a banana you have already peeled off a strip. Later, your child can also try a satsuma (Mandarin orange).

When? 1 year and up.
Time needed:
5 Minutes
Preparation: Easy
What does this support? Fine motor skills, pincer grip, autonomy, attention
Materials: Bananas or satsumas

When? 1 year and up.
Time needed:
5 Minutes
Preparation: Easy
What does this support? Autonomy

CHOOSING CLOTHES

Set out two outfits for your child the evening before, from which your child can choose one the next morning. A larger selection could overwhelm your child.

PRACTICING POURING

At this stage, your child can already practice pou-ring. Do not choose a small glass at first, but one with a larger diameter. The jug should be as small as possible and not completely full, so it does not become too heavy.

When? 1 year and up.
Time needed:
5 Minutes
Preparation: Easy
What does this sup-port?
Fine motor skills, attention, concentration, autonomy
Materials: Large glass, small jug

When? 1 year and up.
Time needed: 5 Minutes
Preparation: Easy
What does this support?
Autonomy, gross motor skil-ls, understanding of growth processes in nature

GARDENING

Let your child help you with gardening. Your child can shovel soil, plant something, pick tomatoes from the bush, water with a small children's watering can, etc.

TAKING OFF SOCKS

You can introduce your child to independent dressing and undressing step by step. Socks are an appropriate first step. Initially, you can help your child remove the socks by pulling the sock over the heel. Small children, like those who have already had their first birthday, will experience a sense of achievement.

When? 1 year and up.
What does this support?
Fine motor skills, autonomy

1 - 1.5 YEARS

PRACTICAL LIFE EXERCISES

18 MONTHS TO TWO YEARS

Motor development: Your child can now walk, run, hop, and throw or kick a ball independently. They are learning to climb stairs by holding onto the handrail. Your child can build sturdy towers and undress with help.

Your child has a great urge to move. Go to playgrounds. Follow this and go for lots of walks in the fresh air.

Language development: Your child understands simple words and phrases and can comply with two-part requests ("Please go to the living room and get your doll."). At almost 2 years old, many children can speak 50 words and form 2-word sentences. They answer questions and can name different parts of the body.

Do not use baby talk; give your child opportunities to speak. Repeat new words several times in different contexts, but do not ask your child to repeat words..

Cognitive and relational development: Your child imitates other people and simulates everyday activities. Your child can easily find familiar objects and solves simple puzzles. Your child recognizes themselves in the mirror and uses their first names to name themselves. Your child fluctuates between attachment behavior (seeking closeness to parents) and exploration (exploring the environment and wanting to be independent).

Involve your child in many everyday activities. Offer them simple puzzles.

HAND-EYE-COORDINATION

FISHING WOODEN PEARLS WITH A PAIR OF HANDY SCOOPERS

Pour water into a shallow tub and put in wooden beads, marbles, or pompoms. In addition, offer your child a pair of handy scoopers and an empty bowl. Show your child how to fish for a bead with the scoopers, then place it in the bowl. Invite your child to continue the exercise.

When? 18 months and up.
Time needed: 5 Minutes
Preparation: Easy
What does this support? Scissor movement and hand-eye-coordination
Materials: Tub, pearls or similar, bowl, handy scoopers

When? 18 months and up.
Time needed: 15 Minutes
Preparation: Easy
What does this support? Scissor movement
Materials: Toilet roll, pen, wiggly eyes if desired, colored paper, glue, scissors

CUTTING A TOILET ROLL'S HAIR

Paint eyes on an empty toilet roll; wiggly eyes glued on look especially funny. Cut out strips of colored paper about 6 cm in length. The strips should be between 5 and 10 mm wide. Glue the strips into the top of the toilet roll as hair from the inside. Now you can cut the hair on the toilet roll together with your child.

THREADING

Tie a double or triple knot in a shoelace. The reinforced end means it works well as a string for threading. Place the shoelace on a tray, together with objects for threading, in a container. Wooden beads, raw pasta with a hole (for example, rigatoni), or muesli in the shape of a ring are suitable. Your child can eat the latter as a snack afterward.

When? 18 months and up.
Time needed: 5 Minutes
Preparation: Easy
What does this support? Hand-eye motor skills and the pincer grip
Materials: Shoelaces, tray, container, wooden beads or noodles

When? 18 months and up.
Time needed: 5 Minutes
Preparation: Easy
What does this support? Fine motor skills
Materials: Modeling clay, wooden sticks, or matches

A MODELING CLAY HEDGEHOG

Roll out a large ball of modeling clay and shape a snout and eyes. This will be your hedgehog. Offer your child small wooden sticks, matches, or toothpicks with the tip removed for this, and stick them into the modeling clay until it has enough spikes.

TURNING NUTS ONTO LARGE SCREWS

Place large screws with matching nuts on a tray. Show your child how to screw the nuts onto the screws and leave it to them to continue this exercise.

When? 18 months and up.
Time needed: 5 Minutes
Preparation: Easy
What does this support? Fine motor skills, turning motions with the fingers
Materials: Screws and nuts, tray

FORMS AND COLORS

When? 18 months and up.

Time needed: 10 Minutes

Preparation: Easy

What does this support? Size perception, concentration

Materials: Lids, paper, pen

ORDERING LIDS BY SIZE

Collect 5 to 7 differently sized lids from screw-top jars. Draw the outline of the lids on a sheet of paper. Offer your child the sheet with the lids on a tray and ask them to match the tops to their outlines. Demonstrate this with a lid, and your child should be able to independently complete the remainder.

COLORED STICKERS

Draw 4 or 5 different colored balloons on a sheet of paper and offer this to your child on a tray with stickers of matching colors. Ask your child to stick the stickers onto the balloons of the same color.

When? 18 months and up.

Time needed: 10 Minutes

Preparation: Easy

What does this support? Color perception, fine motor skills, sorting

Materials: Paper, pen, stickers, tray

COLOR MIX

When? 18 months and up.

Time needed: 10 Minutes

Preparation: Easy

What does this support? Color perception, recognizing mixed colors

Materials: Zip bag, acrylic paint

For this exercise, you need 3 zip bags. Fill each with two acrylic colors (about one tablespoon each). The combinations yellow/red, blue/yellow, and red/blue are suitable. The blobs of color should not touch each other in the bags. Close the bags and attach them to a window. Your child can then mix the colors to their heart's content by squeezing the bags with their hands. This creates different mixed colors from the basic colors contained in the bags.

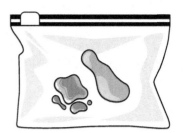

DRIPPING WITH PIPETTES

Fill small glasses with water and put a few squirts of food coloring in each glass so that each container is colored differently. Offer your child cotton pads and pipettes and show them how to use the pipettes to drip water onto the pads. Your child will enjoy doing this activity.

When? 18 months and up.

Time needed: 5 Minutes

Preparation: Easy

What does this support? Color perception, fine motor skills, concentration

Materials: Glasses, water, food coloring, cotton pads, pipettes

When? 18 months and up.

Time needed: 10 Minutes

Preparation: Easy

What does this support? Color perception, sorting things

Materials: Egg carton, colors, basket, squeeze pouch lids

SORTING SQUEEZE POUCH LIDS BY COLOR

Paint the wells of an empty egg carton with different colors. Place the carton on a tray with a basket of matching squeeze pouch lids (or pompoms). Ask your child to put the lids in the matching well. You can show them how to do it, and they should be able to independently complete the remainder.

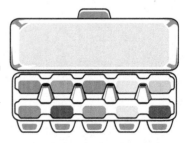

LANGUAGE AND LISTENING

EMOTION CARDS

Browse the Internet for pictures of children going through strong emotions (joy, anger, sadness, etc.). Print them out, laminate them, and round the corners. Alternatively, you can buy emotion cards or templates for them from online stores. Use the cards and ask your child how they think the children in the pictures feel. Talk to your child about their emotional state after they have experienced strong feelings such as anger or sadness.

When? 18 months and up.
Time needed: 20 Minutes
Preparation: Medium
What does this support? Vocabulary, expressing emotions
Materials: Printed and laminated pictures

FINDING THE RIGHT FIGURE

When? 18 months and up.
Time needed: 20 Minutes
Preparation: Medium
What does this support? Vocabulary, concentration
Materials: Animal figures, blanket, basket

Pick out 6 to 9 of your child's animal figures or small vehicles and find a corresponding picture for each figure. Print them out individually and laminate them. Place them on a small blanket (this delimits the child's working area) and name the figures depicted. Now offer your child a small basket with the corresponding animals and show them how to match the 3D objects to the 2D pictures. The exercise becomes more difficult if the depicted cards also show the environment of the animals, for example, the desert or trees.

SEARCHING GAME IN NATURE

On a walk with your child, look for typical natural materials that fit the season, for example, chestnuts, moss, beechnuts, stones, a stream or river, etc. Either photograph these things secretly or look for pictures of them on the Internet. Print the photos or images and arrange on a page and laminate them. Go on a discovery mission with your child in nature and look for everything pictured. Name them and tick off the objects found, or collect them and match them to the pictures at home.

When? 18 months and up.
Time needed: 20 Minutes
Preparation: Medium
What does this support? Vocabulary, attention
Materials: Printed photographs

When? 18 months and up.
Time needed: 20 Minutes
Preparation: Medium
What does this support? Vocabulary
Materials: Printed photographs

SEARCHING GAME AT HOME

Take photos of familiar objects in your home (for example, your child's favorite toys, shoes or jacket, plate, etc.). Your child should be able to reach all these things easily. Print out the photos and show them to your child one by one. Ask your child what they see in the picture and ask them to pick up the item in question. Your child will try to name as many objects as possible.

WEATHER STATION

Make a weather station from one side of an old shipping box by drawing a frame. Draw weather symbols on paper (sunny, cloudy, rain, windy, snow, rainbow), cut them out as a circle, and laminate the cards. Put Velcro dots on the bottoms of the cards and make sure they stick to the weather station. Check the weather every morning together with your child and hang up the appropriate card.

When? 18 months and up.
Time needed: 20 Minutes
Preparation: Medium
What does this support? Vocabulary, perception of environmental stimuli
Materials: Pens, shipping box, Velcro dots

TOUCH

COLORED RICE

When? 18 months and up.
Time needed: 10 Minutes
Preparation: Easy
What does this support? Sense of touch, color perception
Materials: Rice, freezer bag, food coloring, tub

Fill a freezer bag with raw rice and add a few dashes of food coloring. Close the bag and knead everything well until the rice is evenly colored. Let the rice dry overnight or put it in the oven at 50 degrees for 10 minutes. Offer your child rice in different colors in a shallow tub for them to play with.

WATER AND OIL

Fill a zip bag with water colored with food coloring. Add a few drops of oil. Close the bag tightly and offer it to your child to play with. Your child will move the oil by pushing it around.

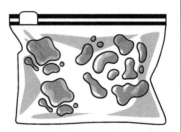

When? 18 months and up.
Time needed: 5 Minutes
Preparation: Easy
What does this support? Color perception, sense of touch
Materials: Food coloring, water, zip bag, oil

BAKING POWDER VOLCANOS

When? 18 months and
up.
Time needed:
10 Minutes
Preparation: Easy
What does this support? Sense for experimentation
Materials: Baking powder, tub, glasses, food coloring, water, vinegar, tweezers

Pour a thin layer of baking powder into a shallow tub. Prepare a few jars by putting a few drops of food coloring in each jar and filling them with one-third water and two-thirds full of vinegar. Offer the differently colored jars to your child along with some tweezers and drizzle a few drops onto the baking soda. It will become colorful, fizz, and bubble.

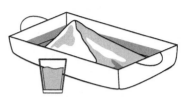

KINETIC SAND

Mix flour and oil in a ratio of 8:1 (8 cups flour to 1 cup oil). Add glitter or food coloring if desired and mix thoroughly. Offer the kinetic sand to your child in a shallow tub to knead and play with.

When? 18 months and
up.
Time needed:
10 Minutes
Preparation: Easy
What does this support? Sense of touch, hand muscles
Materials: Flour, oil, food coloring

LEAF PRINTS

When? 18 months and
up.
Time needed:
5 Minutes
Preparation: Easy
What does this support? Sense of touch, fine motor skills
Materials: Leaves, paint, paper

Collect leaves with your child during a walk. Let them dry at home. Coat one side with paint and press it onto paper. Make leaf prints together with your child and compare them.

TOUCH

18 M. - 2 YEARS

THINKING TRAINING

RECOGNIZING ANIMAL PRINTS IN DOUGH

Roll out salt dough or self-hardening modeling clay with a rolling pin. Cut out some circles with a glass. Take your child's playing figures and make a few footprints on a circle with one playing figure at a time. Repeat this with the rest of the figures. Let the mass harden, and offer your child the circles and figures on a tray. Ask your child to match the footprints to the individual animals.

Recipe for the salt dough: Mix two cups of flour with one cup of water and one cup of salt. Knead the dough. If it sticks to your hands, add a little more flour.

When? 18 months and up.
Time needed: 15 Minutes
Preparation: Medium
What does this support? Pattern recognition, attention, concentration
Materials: Flour, water, salt, cups, rolling pin, glass, playing figures, tray

When? 18 months and up.
Time needed: 10 Minutes
Preparation: Easy
What does this support? Concentration, attention, pattern recognition, logical thinking
Materials: Beads, string, pictures, tray

THREADING BEADS ACCORDING TO A PATTERN TEMPLATE

Pick out some differently colored beads and a suitable string to thread on (for example, a shoelace). Thread on different patterns and take pictures of them. Print out the pictures, laminate them, and round off the corners. Put the pictures on a tray together with the beads and the string, and ask your child to thread the patterns. Start with only three different colored beads at the beginning.

SAVING ANIMAL FIGURES

Wrap several rubber bands around the individual links of a plate holder. Place animal figures or small toy vehicles in the tangled stretchy material and encourage your child to free the figures. Don't be afraid to tangle them up.

When? 18 months and up.
Time needed: 5 Minutes
Preparation: Easy
What does this support? Concentration, action planning, fine motor skills
Materials: Rubber bands, plate holders, animal figures

ARRANGING LEGOS AFTER A PATTERNTO A PATTERN TEMPLATE

When? 21 months and up.
Time needed: 20 Minutes
Preparation: Medium
What does this support? Concentration, attention, pattern recognition
Materials: Lego bricks, tray

Take two to three different colored large Lego bricks and stick them together. Take a photo of these shapes. Alternatively, you can create the templates on your PC and color them in or sketch them on paper and color them in. Laminate the templates and round off the corners. Offer your child the templates together with the necessary bricks on a tray. Ask your child to copy the patterns. Once your child is older, you can make the patterns more difficult.

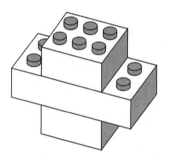

WHAT GOES TOGETHER?

Find pictures on the Internet of pairs that go together, for example, trousers/jacket, fork/knife, male animal/female animal. Spread all the pairs on a tray and ask your child to look for pairs that go together. You can show them how to do this with one pair and help them if your child still finds this task difficult.

When? 21 months and up.
Time needed: 20 Minutes
Preparation: Medium
What does this support? Abstract thinking, concentration, attention
Materials: Tray, pictures

PRACTICAL LIFE EXERCISES

When? 18 months and up.
Time needed: 5 Minutes
Preparation: Easy
What does this support? Fine motor skills, self-efficacy
Materials: Wave cutter, fruit, vegetables

CUTTING WITH A WAVE CUTTER

Let your child chop up fruit and vegetables with a wave cutter. Bananas, for instance, are well suited for this. This way, your child can prepare a snack for themselves.

PLANTING AND WATERING CRESS

Plant cress together with your child and water it regularly. Your child will be fascinated by the growing plants.

When? 18 months and up.
Time needed: 5 Minutes
Preparation: Easy
What does this support? Understanding natural processes, caring for others
Materials: Cress

108

SCALES

When? 18 months and up.
Time needed: 5 Minutes
Preparation: Easy
What does this support? Understanding of weight
Materials: Analogue scales, various toys

Get your child a classic analog scale with two weighing pans. Place several toys into the pans. Weigh the two pans separately to find out which is heavier. This way, your child can experiment at their own pace.

ARRANGING FLOWERS

Collect flowers and herbs with your child in your garden or during a walk. Offer your child a small carafe or jar to arrange the flowers independently. Then place the flowers on the common dining table or your child's table.

When? 18 months and up.
Time needed: 10 Minutes
Preparation: Easy
What does this support? Concentration, fine motor skills
Materials: Flowers, herbs, carafe or glass

TIME OF THE YEAR TABLE

When? 18 months and up.
Time needed: 15 Minutes
Preparation: Medium
What does this support? Understanding of seasons
Materials: Side table or stool, various materials

Set up a small corner in your home that you decorate with your child to match the season. This can be a small wall shelf at your child's height, a small side table, or a stool. You can use natural materials, colored silk scarves, and small figures (for example, made of felt). Your imagination is the limit here.

TWO TO THREE YEARS

~

Motor development: Your child can now safely walk, run, hop, and climb stairs. They can walk on tiptoe, run towards a goal and slow down in time, kick, throw, and perhaps even catch a ball. They are learning to pedal, pull toys towards them, and carry heavier things.

Your child can now draw a circle and screw lids on and off. They can turn knobs and operate switches.

Language development: There is a vocabulary explosion, and your child learns new words daily. The sentences become increasingly complex, and the pronunciation is increasingly more understandable, even for strangers. Your child begins to ask questions. The grammar is already correct in many places (for example, "I am going," "he is going"). However, your child still makes mistakes, especially in plural or past tense. Around the second birthday, your child no longer refers to themselves by their first name but uses the pronoun "I." At the age of 3, your child can briefly recount experiences and enhance them with filler words such as adjectives.

Cognitive and relational development: The child is beginning to understand and recognize themselves as a person. They know their gender and hair color and that they are part of an environment. The child shows empathy and compassion. The third year of life marks the beginning of the magical phase, i.e., the belief in fantastical beings. The child also assumes that their words, thoughts, and actions can cause or prevent events. Many children have separation anxiety at this age, so parents should be sensitive. With many tantrums and the desire for independence, the autonomy phase is also a challenge for the whole family, which you can counteract with as much participation as possible in everyday life..

HAND·EYE· COORDINATION

DRAWING DOTS WITH COTTON BUDS

In addition to classical painting, you can offer your child a change of pace with entirely different materials. If you are artistically talented, you can draw a simple picture with a pencil and trace the lines with a thin felt-tip pen. The dots should not be too far apart. Of course, you can also print out the picture and trace it.

Offer the dot pictures to your child together with paint and cotton balls. Your child can now dab the dots with the cotton. This exercise is particularly suitable as a seasonal activity. You can easily adapt the motifs to the season (for example, a winter snowflake or a summer popsicle).

When? 2 years and up.
Time needed: 15 Minutes
Preparation: Easy
What does this support? Fine motor skills, correct pen position, concentration
Materials: Pencil, paper, felt-tip pen, paint, cotton buds

When? 2 years and up.
Time needed: 10 Minutes
Preparation: Easy
What does this support? Fine motor skills, concentration, endurance
Materials: Glue, paper, pen

TRACING A LINE WITH CUTTINGS

Toddlers usually like making things with glue. You can draw a line on a piece of paper. Your child can then glue paper scraps along the line. You can easily vary the difficulty of this exercise by making snaking lines or a spiral instead of a straight line. You can offer your child ready-made paper scraps (paper scraps from other craft activities can be used for this), or your child can cut them into small pieces or tear them off themselves.

2 - 3 YEARS

PLACING MARBLES ON LEGO BRICKS

If you have marbles and Lego Duplo at home, you can combine the two in a nice fine motor exercise. Offer your child a larger building block (for example, with 2x4 pegs) and marbles on an action tray. There should be as many marbles as there are pegs; for instance, eight marbles for eight pegs. You can place a marble on a peg to show your child the possible activity. You will notice that putting all the marbles on the Lego brick is difficult without knocking another one down again. Although your child has previously mastered the pincer grip, this exercise is challenging. You can vary this activity by offering different colored building blocks with marbles of matching colors. This creates a small color-sorting training at the same time.

When? 2 years and up.
Time needed: 5 Minutes
Preparation: Easy
What does this support? Fine motor skills, pincer grip, concentration
Materials: Marbles, Lego Duplo, Tray

CUTTING ALONG LINES

At age two, most children are enthusiastic about cutting with scissors. There are special children's scissors that are easy to use and only cut paper. You can leave these to your child without worrying about hair, clothing, or home textiles.

When? 2 years and up.
Time needed: 5 Minutes
Preparation: Easy
What does this support? Dexterity, fine motor skills, attention
Materials: Children's scissors, paper, pen

Once your child understands the concept of cutting, you can help them perfect this skill. Cut a sheet of paper (not cardboard) into 2 cm wide and 15 cm long strips. You can now mark these strips with lines for your child to cut along. Do not draw the lines lengthwise, but across so your child can cut off a piece with one cut. The easiest way is to draw horizontal lines about 2 cm apart. Diagonal strokes are more difficult. If your child is already more experienced in this activity, you can reduce the distance between the strokes. You can reuse the snippets for other activities, for example, the gluing exercise mentioned earlier.

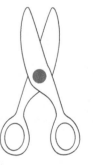

PLACING POMPOMS IN AN EGG CARTON WITH TWEEZERS

Using tweezers requires fine motor skills and strengthens the muscles in the hands. Please do not use pointed tweezers, but a large variety made of wood or plastic that your child can easily grasp with their small hands. You can offer your child an empty egg carton, pompoms, and tweezers on a tray and demonstrate how to transfer the pompoms into the egg carton with the tweezers. You can also turn this exercise into a sorting activity by painting the wells of the egg carton in different colors and offering pompoms in matching shades.

When? 2.5 years and up.
Time needed: 5 Minutes
Preparation: Easy
What does this support? Fine motor skills, hand muscles
Materials: Tweezers, egg carton, pompoms

When? 2 years and up.
Time needed: 15 Minutes
Preparation: Easy
What does this support? Fine motor skills, correct pen holding
Materials: Cardboard, paper, pen, adhesive tape

FIRST WRITING EXERCISES

You can offer your child their first writing exercises from about two and a half years old. There are many books with different levels of difficulty for this activity. Especially for small children who still miss a few things, you can easily do the exercises yourself. Take a piece of cardboard and stick a sheet on it. Draw the lines on this sheet that your child is supposed to follow.

To begin with, choose lines that are as simple as possible without too many curves. Then cover the page with clear parcel tape, adhesive tape, or sticky bookbinding paper. Your child can now do the writing exercises with a felt-tip pen, which can be easily wiped away afterward.

TARGET PRACTICE WITH A BALL

This activity is sure to be a lot of fun for your child. Sit your child down at a table (a small children's table is best). On the opposite side of the table, cardboard cups are taped side by side so that their top edge is aligned with the table, and there is no space between the cups. Your child can try to make a small ball or marble roll across the table so that it hits a cup at the end. Of course, they have to use their strength in a controlled way so they don't overshoot the target. You can play with your child and compete to see who gets the most hits.

When? 2.5 years and up.

Time needed: 5 Minutes

Preparation: Easy

What does this support? Attention, concentration, fine motor skills, ability to target

Materials: Paper cup, adhesive tape, small ball

FORMS AND COLORS

PUZZLES WITH WOODEN STICKS

This activity is an alternative to classic puzzles. It is best suited for a visit to a restaurant or a train journey due to the very small pack size. You will need the following:

- Wooden tongue depressor or spatula (like the ones used at the doctor's office)
- Masking tape or adhesive tape
- A printed image of choice
- Glue
- A box cutter or scalpel

Place the wooden spatulas next to each other and fix them together with a piece of masking or adhesive tape. Turn the spatulas over and stick a picture on them. Get creative! You can print an image from your child's favorite series, photos of family members, or picture pages from discarded books. If you have single-sided adhesive label paper at home, you can print the image and stick it onto the wooden spatulas. Now turn the spatulas over, remove the masking or adhesive tape, and carefully cut the individual spatulas apart with the box cutter. Your child is sure to have lots of fun putting the picture together.

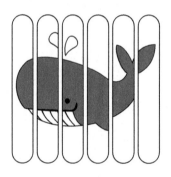

When? 2 years and up.
Time needed: 15 Minutes
Preparation: Easy
What does this support? Attention, concentration
Materials: Wooden spatula, masking tape, glue, scalpel

CYLINDER BLOCKS

Cylinder blocks are a classic Montessori learning toy available in various online stores. These consist of (usually four) different blocks with different cylinders to insert. Each block has a different focus. Sometimes the cylinders are all the same height but have different diameters, sometimes, the diameters are the same, but the cylinders are different heights and need to be arranged so that they all end up at the same height.

You should offer your child only one cylinder block on a tray to get started. Put the individual cylinders in a small basket on the tray. Once your child has become more confident in this exercise, you can put different blocks (eventually all of them) together on the tray. It is a good idea to make sure that all the cylinders have the same color when buying them so that you can also offer the highest difficulty level.

When? 2 years and up.
What does this support? Understanding of hollow spaces, volumes, sequences, and structures

When? 2 years and up.
Time needed: 10 Minutes
Preparation: Easy
What does this support? Size perception, attention, concentration
Materials: Cardboard, scissors, paper, tray, container

SIZE DIFFERENCES IN SHAPES

Cut out different-sized shapes from a piece of cardboard or construction paper, for example, seven differently-sized triangles. Outline these shapes on a white sheet of paper so that all the outlines are visible at the end. Place the sheet on a tray and offer the cut-out shapes in a separate container. Let your child match the shapes to the respective outline. This will give your child a sense of different sizes for the same shape. You can increase the difficulty by combining different shapes. The shapes can also be hidden in a sensory tub, for example, under lentils or colored rice, so your child must look for them and match them up.

When? 2 years and up.
Time needed:
5 Minutes
Preparation: Easy
What does this support? Color recognition, sorting, correct pen holding
Materials: Felt-tip pens, paper

CONNECTING COLORED DOTS

Use a felt-tip pen to draw dots in different colors in a circle on a sheet of paper. Make sure to use each color exactly twice. Your child can now connect the same colors.

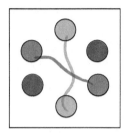

FORMS AND COLORS

DISCOVERING SHADES OF COLORS

At this point, your child knows the basic colors and can probably confidently name them. You can also familiarize your child with other color tones and shades. You can get small color cards free of charge at your local hardware store. These have individual color shades. Cut the color cards apart so that the unique colors are separated. Punch a small hole in each color card with a hole punch or hole punch pliers. Glue these dots onto small wooden pegs and let your child put the pegs on the corresponding cards.

When? 2.5 years and up.
Time needed:
5 Minutes
Preparation: Easy
What does this support? Understanding color nuances, fine motor skills
Materials: Color cards, scissors, hole punch, wooden clip

When? 2.5 years and up.
Time needed:
5 Minutes
Preparation: Easy
What does this support? Perception of shapes
Materials: Paper, pen, container, tray

LEARNING SHAPES

Let your child sort different shapes. Start with the classic shapes of circles, triangles, and squares. Draw each shape on a small sheet of paper. Put three small containers on a tray. You can use empty, flat yogurt pots for this, for example. Place one of the sheets in each container. Now you only need corresponding shapes that your child can sort into. You can cut these shapes out of hard craft cardboard in different colors or use the wooden shapes from a hammer game.

2 – 3 YEARS

118

LANGUAGE AND LISTENING

LISTENING MEMORY

Fill various materials into similar-looking, opaque containers (e.g., film canisters) using sand, rice, water, a bead, or a material of your preference. Fill two containers with the same substance. Your child should now identify the matching ones based only on the sound. You will be surprised how challenging it is to rely solely on the sense of hearing for such an assignment. It becomes even more difficult if you make a memory game out of it. However, this is more suitable for older children.

When? 2 years and up.
Time needed:
10 Minutes
Preparation: Easy
What does this support? Hearing
Materials: Cans, rice, water, or other things

When? 2 years and up.
Time needed:
15 Minutes
Preparation: Easy
What does this support? Vocabulary
Materials: Cardboard, pen

SHOPPING LIST

If your child has a toy shop or a play kitchen with different ingredients, you can vary the shopping game by preparing other shopping lists for your child. For this, draw the corresponding ingredients on a piece of cardboard (or stick them on a corresponding printout) and let your child go shopping with this list. In doing so, your child will learn the names of the food items shown and, at the same time, act out a situation that is relevant to everyday life.

ASSIGNING INITIAL SOUNDS

Print out cards of things that have the same initial sound (for example, mouse - moon - monkey, ant - arm - apple) and let your child find the cards with the same sound. You can help your child with this exercise by speaking the words aloud and emphasizing the initial sounds particularly clearly. It would be best to make these cards durable by laminating them or using bookbinding foil.

When? 2 years and up.
Time needed:
5 Minutes
Preparation: Easy
What does this support?
Materials: Printed cards

When? 2.5 years and up.
Time needed:
20 Minutes
Preparation: Easy
What does this support? Understanding of language
Materials: Printed out pictures of rhyming objects, cardboard

RECOGNIZING RHYMING PAIRS

Your child is already familiar with nursery rhymes from infancy and many songs and books. You can now deepen their linguistic understanding by having them match rhyming pairs. Print pictures of rhyming objects (e.g., house - mouse, cat - bat, tree - bee). Make them durable by laminating them or sticking them on cardboard and covering them with transparent tape or bookbinding foil. Start with very few pairs of words at the beginning, for example, only 6 different pictures. You can increase the number over time.

TOUCH

WATER BEADS

Water beads are very popular with almost all children. Prepare an action tub for your child with different kitchen objects, for example, a funnel, spoons, ladles, or even handy scoopers, and just let your child play with the beads.

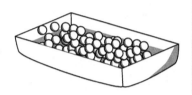

When? 2 years and up.
What does this support? Sense of touch
Materials: Water beads, tub, kitchen objects

When? 2 years and up.
Time needed: 5 Minutes
Preparation: Easy
What does this support? Fine motor skills, hand muscles, action planning
Materials: Toy animals, water, tub, container, pipette

ANIMAL FIGURES ON ICE

This activity is especially suitable for warm summer days. Freeze your child's toy animals overnight in small containers. The animals should be completely covered with water. You can also color the water with food coloring. Remove the frozen animals from the container the next day and offer them to your child in a tub. In addition, add a container with warm water and a pipette. You can also provide a spray bottle with warm water. Make sure that the water is not hot. Your child can now free the animals from the ice with these tools.

121

MAGIC BAG

Place an object your child is familiar with in a cloth bag (for example, a toy or fruit). Have your child identify this object with the sense of touch by reaching into the bag.

When? 2 years and up.
Time needed:
5 Minutes
Preparation: Easy
What does this support? Sense of touch
Materials: Cloth bag, toy

BAREFOOT PATH

You can create a small barefoot path with your child if you have a garden. Separate small squares from each other with small wooden beams and fill them with different materials, for example, sand, grass, moss, coarse stones, or gravel. If you don't have a garden, you can create something similar indoors with your child. Cut larger pieces of the same size from old cardboard boxes and glue on different materials with a hot glue gun, for example, a grass mat, different fabrics, pipe cleaners laid side by side, tightly laid pompoms, etc. Your child can walk over it with bare feet.

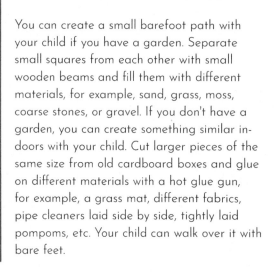

When? 2 years and up.
Time needed:
1 Hour
Preparation: Medium
What does this support? Sensory perception with the feet
Materials: Wooden beams, natural materials, hot glue gun

DRAWING WITH SALT

You will need glue, black construction paper, salt, food coloring, and a pipette for this activity. Have your child pre-paint a picture with the glue and sprinkle plenty of salt over it. Shake off the excess salt and let it dry. Then your child can drip food coloring onto the salt with a pipette to color it in. An exceptional work of art!

When? 2 years and up.
Time needed:
5 Minutes
Preparation: Easy
What does this support? Fine motor skills
Materials: Glue, clay paper, salt, food coloring, pipette

When? 2 years and up.
Time needed:
5 Minutes
Preparation: Easy
What does this support? Sense of touch
Materials: Different fabrics, pieces of wood, glue

FEELING MEMORY

For a feeling memory, you need different fabrics and pieces of wood of the same size or small wooden bowls. You can use different materials from your home, for example, sandpaper, jeans, velvet, wool, or mirror foil. Stick the same fabric on the bottom of two pieces of wood and try to find matching pairs together with your child. It gets more difficult when you change it into a memory game.

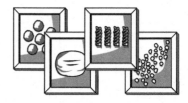

THINKING TRAINING

RECOGNIZING ANIMAL BABIES

Look for pictures of animals and their babies on the Internet. Print them on cards, laminate them, and let your child find the cards that go together. This will consolidate your child's vocabulary. At the same time, you can mix in more difficult pairs, for example, tadpole and frog, fish spawn, and fish or caterpillar and butterfly.

When? 2 years and up.
Time needed:
15 Minutes
Preparation: Easy
What does this support? Knowledge about animals
Materials: Printed-out animal pictures

LOTTERY GAME

When? 2 years and up.
Time needed:
15 Minutes
Preparation: Easy
What does this support? Attention, concentration, memory
Materials: Printed pictures, scissors

Make a lottery game. For this, you need 6 different pictures for each player. Print out these pictures twice in two rows, one below the other. One of these prints at a time will now become your game board. Make it durable by laminating it or with bookbinding foil. You can cut up the second printout. Laminate the individual cards as well. Each player receives a board, and the individual playing cards are placed upside down between the players. Each player, in turn, may turn over one card. If they locate the picture on their game board, they can place the card over that image (like a game piece). If the card does not belong to their board, they put it back face down.

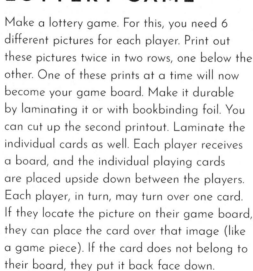

124

THREADING ACCORDING TO COLOR

Thread different colored beads and take a photo of them. Print them out, laminate the cards, and let your child thread the bead necklace according to the template. For this, offer the cards, the thread, and the beads used.

When? 2.5 years and up.
Time needed: 5 Minutes
Preparation: Easy
What does this support? Fine motor skills, pattern recognition
Materials: Beads, thread, printed pictures

When? 2.5 years and up.
Time needed: 20 Minutes
Preparation: Easy
What does this support? Pattern recognition, action planning, concentration, attention
Materials: Pompoms, Pop-It, printed pictures, tray

SORTING POMPOMS INTO POP-ITS

If your child has a Pop-It, you can use it to teach them to follow patterns. Put pompoms in different places in the Pop-It. It is easier if you only use pompoms of the same color, so your child only has to find the corresponding position in the Pop-It. It becomes more difficult if you also use different colored pompoms. Take a photo of the Pop-It with the pompoms. Repeat this in different variations, print the pictures, and make them resistant with a laminator or bookbinding foil. Place the pictures with the used pompoms and the Pop-It on a tray and let your child copy the patterns.

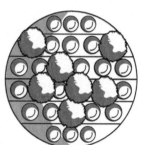
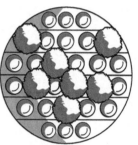

ASSEMBLE LEGO ACCORDING TO INSTRUCTIONS

From about two and a half years old, your child can assemble simple building block structures according to instructions. Take photos of Lego or building blocks put together in different ways. Print them out, laminate them, and offer the patterns together with the necessary bricks. Your child can now try to recreate the designs.

When? 2.5 years and up.
Time needed: 15 Minutes
Preparation: Easy
What does this support? Pattern recognition
Materials: Legos or building blocks, printed pictures

2 - 3 YEARS

125

WOODEN SPATULA WITH DOT STICKERS

When? 2.5 years and up.
Time needed: 15 Minutes
Preparation: Easy
What does this support? Pattern recognition
Materials: Wooden spatula, dot stickers, boxcutter

You only need wooden spatulas, dot stickers, and a box cutter for this exercise. Place two wooden spatulas next to each other and stick several dot stickers in the middle of the spatulas. Then cut the spatulas apart so that only half of the dot stickers are visible on each spatula. Repeat this with different patterns. Your child can now find the matching wooden spatulas and assemble the patterns.

COUNTING

Some children can already count to ten at the age of two. However, they usually only learn this sequence of numbers by heart and do not yet have a real understanding of quantities. You can encourage this with this exercise and also introduce the numbers. To do this, you need some flat empty containers, for example, wooden or plastic bowls or simply flat empty yogurt pots. Place a piece of paper with a number on it in the container and draw the corresponding number of dots underneath. Offer your child the containers with pompoms (alternatively beads, marbles, or similar). Have your child put the corresponding number of pompoms in the respective container. Feel free to help your child count them.

When? 2.5 years and up.
Time needed: 5 Minutes
Preparation: Easy
What does this support? Number and quantity comprehension, number recognition
Materials: Empty containers, small pieces of paper, pen, pompoms

PRACTICAL LIFE EXERCISES

POURING

Your child has already experienced pouring exercises and is probably quite confident in filling their glass from a small jug. You can help your child perfect this skill. Position four to five glasses next to each other on a tray. Draw a horizontal line around each glass (at a different height for each glass). Your child should now pour the water up to this line. Doing this on a tiled surface is best in case something goes wrong. This good motor exercise will make your child's daily routine easier.

When? 2 years and up.
Time needed:
5 Minutes
Preparation: Easy
What does this support? Pouring, concentration, fine motor skills, autonomy
Materials: Glasses, tray

BAKING TOGETHER

Toddlers love to help with cooking and baking. You can bake a cake with your child and increase their autonomy by providing a prepared environment. Fill the required quantities into individual bowls beforehand. If your child is already very confident in pouring, you can also make a line on a measuring cup up to which your child should pour milk or water. You can arrange the individual ingredients in rows and number them consecutively. Your child can mix the individual inaredients and whisk them with your help. There are also mechanical whisks that are suitable for children. You can buy baking sets for children in stores, in which baking instructions are shown with pictures and, with appropriately colored measuring spoons, can be followed relatively independently, even by quite young children.

When? 2 years and up.
Time needed:
5 Minutes
Preparation: Easy
What does this support? Autonomy, following steps, fine motor skills
Materials: Ingredients, bowls, whisks

SWEEPING EXERCISE

When? 2 years and up.
Time needed:
5 Minutes
Preparation: Easy
What does this support? Fine motor skills, autonomy
Materials: Masking tape, rice, small broom

If something gets spilled, you can ask your child to help you sweep it up. You can ensure your child learns to sweep purposefully in a dry run. Use masking tape to tape a square of about 20x20 cm on the floor and scatter something next to it that needs to be swept up, for example, rice. Ask your child to sweep it into the square. You can provide your child with a child's broom for this or a small child-sized hand sweeper. Doing the exercise on a larger tray or a shallow tub with a slightly smaller field is also a good idea for the latter.

SIEVING SEASHELLS

Fill a small tub with sand and hide shells and stones in it. Offer your child the tub with a small sieve and an empty container. Your child can only sift out the objects. This requires a controlled movement of the wrist and forearm, which will be somewhat unfamiliar to your child at first.

When? 2 years and up.
Time needed:
5 Minutes
Preparation: Easy
What does this support? Fine motor skills, attention
Materials: Tub, seashells, sieve, stones

BUTTONING

When? 2 years and up.
Time needed:
15 Minutes
Preparation: Easy
What does this support? Fine motor skills
Materials: Felt, buttons, scissors

Your child can already operate various fasteners. However, buttoning is a demanding fine motor task that requires practice. In Montessori education, there are fastener frames with which the children can practice different fasteners. However, these are quite expensive, and to make them yourself requires manual dexterity. Alternatively, you can make buttoning accessible to your child with felt. Take a strip of thicker felt about 5 cm wide and sew on three to four buttons of different sizes. Cut circles out of another piece and cut a slit in it. Your child can now attach the circles to the buttons.

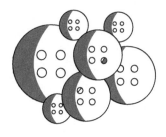

CHILDREN'S KNIFE

Your child can already cut up fruit and vegetables with a wave cutter. You can slowly introduce your child to sharper knives from age two. At first, only use blunt knives, but you can use sharper and sharper ones over time. Let your child help you cook. First, you can use special children's knives that won't damage the skin but can still cut vegetables into small pieces if you apply the right pressure and guide them back and forth. Let your child use the knife only under supervision, and set some rules from the beginning. Knives should not be put in the mouth or licked and should not be waved around wildly.

When? 2.5 years and up.
Time needed: 5 Minutes
Preparation: Easy
What does this support? Number and quantity comprehension, number recognition

SEWING CARDS

You can introduce your toddler to needlework. To do this, draw any (but not too complicated) design on very strong construction paper. Make holes on the design lines at regular intervals with a hole punch. You can show your child how to join the lines using sewing techniques with a blunt plastic needle and wool. Using the pre-punched holes with the design facing front, your child must insert the needle into a hole at the top and then push it through the next hole from the back. Here, the needle is poked through the hole from the bottom up and put back through the first hole to make it a continuous loop. Move on to the next hole. Once the design has been completely sewn, you can cut the thread and knot it on the back. This technique is suitable for making a beautiful birthday card for a loved one with your child. Your child will be very proud of the result. Alternatively, you can also buy corresponding wooden sewing cards online.

When? 2.5 years and up.
Time needed: 10 Minutes
Preparation: Easy
What does this support? Fine motor skills, handicraft skills
Materials: Sturdy construction paper, pen, hole punch, plastic needle, wool

129

FINAL COMMENTS

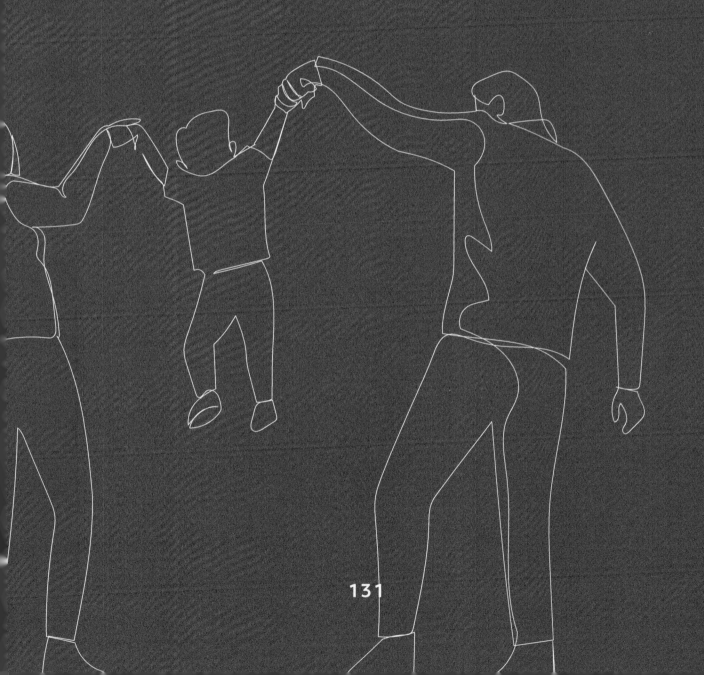

CUSTOMER FEEDBACK

~

Thank you for choosing our book.

We hope it is of great service to you and your child and that you enjoy the activities together.

Feedback and ratings from our customers are very important to us. That way, we can understand what we did well and where we need to work on ourselves. This helps us improve the book and make it more useful for parents and children.

If you are satisfied with your purchase, we would be happy if you were to write a short review on Amazon.

With just 20 seconds of your time, you can greatly help other parents and us. You can simply log in to your Amazon account, select this book and briefly describe what you and your child liked the most.

If you are unsatisfied or have ideas for improvement, please scan this QR code. This will lead you to a form through which you can easily share your suggestions with us - that way, you will greatly help future customers and us.

Thank you very much for your help!

CONCLUSION

FINAL COMMENTS

~

We hope this book's game ideas helped your child be motivated and show self-initiative while learning. Children are naturally curious and like to learn. This wonderful characteristic can be supported and accompanied by the help of well-thought-out materials. Children will retain their love for learning if the learning process is successful. They acknowledge and build on their strengths while respecting and working on their weaknesses. Mistakes are seen as a valuable part of the learning process.

You recognize each child's uniqueness through the constant observation and reflection with which you, as adults, accompany your child's learning process. That way, you can ensure your child can freely develop within the learning process. With learning, you let your child take the lead and are guided by your child's interests and curiosity. But you never leave your child alone but are close by their side, allowing them to learn autonomously.

You help your child become an independent, autonomous, and mature adult who can take responsibility and is aware of their role in society.

At the same time, this book is meant to make you see how precious the first years of your child's life are. This time may be challenging for many parents. Still, it is also full of opportunities, as you can put your child on the right track for the future.

Montessori education is a global movement that is not restricted to the first three years of life. That means you can live by the ways of Montessori without your child attending a special Montessori school or institution. There are many ideas for games or how to decorate your home for older children.

The books *"The Montessori Toddler"* and *"The Montessori Baby"* by Simone Davies can give you more insight. In these books, you will learn about the practical implementation of theoretical groundwork.

You can also find a lot of inspiration online. Pinterest or Instagram are especially well-suited for specialized searches. On Etsy, you will find a plethora of Montessori-related products. With increasing age, your child will move from concrete to more abstract materials; you can, for example, create cards for reading practice and make them more durable by laminating them. And even with older children, you can still create many games at home.

A few highly recommend blogs are *Living Montessori Now*, *Carrots are Orange*, and *The Montessori-Minded Mom*. You can find plenty of materials and useful information for your Montessori journey there.

Stay curious and experience this intense time of learning together with your child. Your child will benefit from your companionship and take charge of their own learning process.

IMPRINT

© TG Edition
1st edition
Author: Maria Stampfer
Contributors: Stefanie Grießl
Design: Similde Mair
All rights reserved.

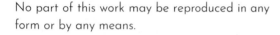

Contact:
TG Edition
Thomas Larch
Feldbauernweg 22
39010 St. Martin in Passeier
Italy
E-mail: support@tg48.de

IMAGE REFERENCES

Cover image: nataliaderiabina - freepik.com
Page 15: freepik.com
Page 19: camomileleyla - freepik.com
Page 77: oksix - freepik.com
graphics page 9, 27, 35, 47, 63, 81, 97, 111, 131:
user4541274 - freepik.com

DISCLAIMER

All information, instructions and strategies contained in this book are used at your own risk. The author cannot be held liable for any damages of any kind for any legal reason.
For damages of a material or non-material nature caused by the use or non-use of the information or use of incorrect and/or incomplete information, any liability claims against the author are excluded. Any legal claims and claims for damages are therefore also excluded.
This work has been compiled and written down with the utmost care. However, the author does not assume any liability for the topicality, completeness and quality of the information. Misprints and incorrect information cannot be completely ruled out. No legal responsibility or liability in any form whatsoever can be accepted for incorrect indications.

Printed in Great Britain
by Amazon

50470593R00077